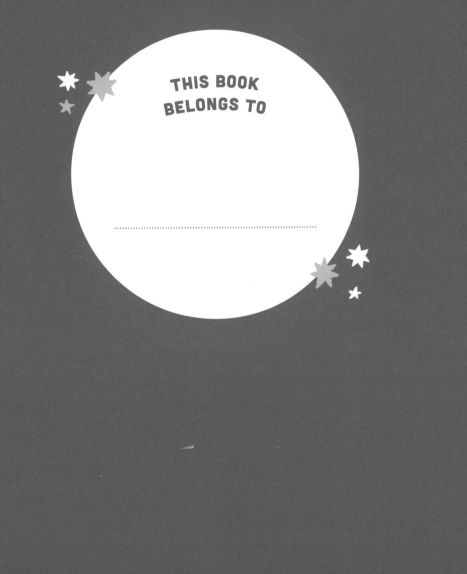

THIS BOOK
BELONGS TO

....

CORE 52

FAMILY EDITION

BUILD KIDS' BIBLE CONFIDENCE in 10 Minutes a Day

written by MARK E. MOORE and MEGAN HOWERTON
illustrated by GRACE HABIB

WATERBROOK

To Jordan Howerton:
The son-in-law I prayed for before Megan was born. Though she wrote this book, you have lived it for my grandchildren.
—Mark

To Jackson, Duke, Lennon, and Dean:
Loving you has given me a deeper understanding about the love of God. I pray you fall more in love with him every day.
—Megan

CORE 52 FAMILY EDITION

Published in the United States by WaterBrook, an imprint of Random House, a division of Penguin Random House LLC.

ISBN 978-0-593-23629-1
EBOOK ISBN 978-0-593-23630-7

The Library of Congress catalog record is available at https://lccn.loc.gov/2021032881.

Printed in China

waterbrookmultnomah.com

10 9 8 7 6 5 4 3 2 1

First Edition

Book design by Sonia Persad
Cover design by Ashley Tucker

CONTENTS

A Note from the Authors 6

WEEK

1 Why Am I Here? GENESIS 1:1 9

2 Who Am I? GENESIS 1:26 13

3 What Is My Problem? GENESIS 3:6 17

4 How Can I Connect with God? GENESIS 15:6 21

5 How Do I Get Right with God? LEVITICUS 11:45 25

6 Is Jesus as Good as They Say? DEUTERONOMY 18:18 29

7 What Is God Looking for in Leaders? 1 SAMUEL 16:7 33

8 Does God Direct History? 2 SAMUEL 7:12 37

9 How Can I Find Happiness? PSALM 1:1–3 41

10 Is There Proof That Jesus Is God's Son? PSALM 2:7 45

11 Is God Really Watching Out for Me? PSALM 23:1–3 50

WEEK

12 Is Jesus a Real Savior? PSALM 110:1 54

13 If Jesus Was Rejected, Why Should I Accept Him? PSALM 118:22 58

14 How Do I Become Wise? PROVERBS 1:7 62

15 How Can Jesus's Death Take Care of My Problems? ISAIAH 53:5 67

16 How Can I Have a Relationship with God? JEREMIAH 31:33–34 71

17 Why Did Jesus Become Human Like Us? DANIEL 7:13 75

18 What Does It Take to Be Happy? MATTHEW 5:11–12 79

19 How Can I Be a Good Person? MATTHEW 5:20 84

20 How Should I Pray? MATTHEW 6:9–13 88

21 Why Does My Money Matter to God? MATTHEW 6:20–21 93

22 What Does a Christian Life Look Like? MATTHEW 7:12 97

23 How Can I Sacrifice Like Jesus? MATTHEW 16:24–25 101

24 Does God Want Me? MATTHEW 22:14 105

25 Is the Supernatural World Actually Real? MATTHEW 25:41 109

26 What's God's Purpose for Me? MATTHEW 28:18–20 113

27 Why Is Christianity Good News? MARK 1:1 117

28 What Does It Mean to Believe? MARK 1:15 121

29 How Can I Find Rest? MARK 2:27–28 125

30 How Can I Be Great? MARK 10:45 129

31 What Does God Care About Most? MARK 12:29–31 133

32 Is Jesus God? JOHN 1:14 137

33 What Is Real Love? JOHN 3:16 141

WEEK		
34	What Does Real Worship Look Like? JOHN 4:24	145
35	What's Up with the Snack During Church? JOHN 6:53	149
36	Can I Know I'm Saved? JOHN 10:28	153
37	What Does the Holy Spirit Do for Me? ACTS 1:8	157
38	Why Did Jesus Leave the Earth? ACTS 1:9	161
39	Why Should I Be Baptized? ACTS 2:38	165
40	What Is God's Solution to Racism? ACTS 17:26	169
41	How Can I Find Freedom? ROMANS 8:1	174
42	How Can I Change? ROMANS 12:2	178
43	How Can I Know God's Will for My Life? 1 CORINTHIANS 2:16	182
44	Did Jesus Really Rise from the Dead? 1 CORINTHIANS 15:14	187
45	What Do I Have to Do to Be Saved? EPHESIANS 2:8	191
46	How Can I Help the Church? EPHESIANS 4:4–7	195
47	Why Is Humility Important? PHILIPPIANS 2:5–7	199
48	How Can I Worry Less? PHILIPPIANS 4:6	203
49	How Can I Find a Mentor? 2 TIMOTHY 2:2	207
50	How Do I Make Sense of the Bible? 2 TIMOTHY 3:16–17	211
51	How Do I Gain Grit? HEBREWS 12:1	215
52	What Will Heaven Be Like? REVELATION 21:3	220

A NOTE FROM THE AUTHORS

PARENTS AND MENTORS,

We know that raising kids can be chaotic. I (Mark) raised a strong-willed child (Megan) who has now given me four world-class grandchildren. One day she was sitting with me in our pool and said, "Dad, I love what *Core 52* is doing for adults, taking them through the mountaintop passages of the Bible in one year. I wish there was something like that for my kids." My reply: "Write it!" She protested that she was unqualified. So I ticked off her résumé: college-trained elementary school teacher, mother of four, pastor's wife, and daughter of a Bible college professor. Well, you hold in your hand the result. What Megan put together is incredible (which you expect me to say). But seriously, when she gave me the first few chapters, I was blown away. . . I said (aloud, I think), "This will actually work!"

With tears in my eyes, I began to imagine parents and mentors like you sitting in a classroom or around a dinner table, having life-altering conversations with your kids. I'm a teacher at heart. My job is to give you what you need to equip your children for the battlefield of life (feel free to "cheat" by grabbing a copy of *Core 52* or *Core 52 Student Edition* for your teens). The biblical principles of this book will empower your kids for spiritual success. If you invest ten to fifteen minutes a day, five days a week, for one year, your child will have a firm foundation in every major principle of the Bible. That's our promise.

No one can do for your child what you can do as a mentor. Megan and I simply and humbly want to offer you this resource, which will support you in making a majestic difference in the spiritual growth of those on whom Jesus placed the highest priority.

KIDS,

Here is how you can help your parents make the most of this experience:

DAY 1 *Read the story to your parents.* It's okay to let them read it if they want to.

DAY 2 *Memorize the verse.* You're going to be better at this than your parents are, so you might want to help them find www.core52.org on their cell phones. There is a three-minute video for each verse to help them memorize it with you. (Secret: you can also find the videos on Vimeo in separate channels: Core52 Lesson and Core52 Memory.)

DAY 3 *Read the passage listed.* It's related to the verse you memorized. To figure out how they're related, you can talk through the questions provided. You need to pick only the one you're most comfortable with. (Parents: The three levels here, and on Days 4 and 5, are intended to get more challenging. You may have several children at different stages of development.)

Level 1 Level 2 Level 3 

DAY 4 *Read this passage too.* It will allow you to see your verse from a different angle.

DAY 5 *This is where it gets really good. We give you important questions to ask your parents and ones for them to ask you as well.* Don't let them off the hook. They need to answer too. Have fun. Your parents are a great gift from God, and the time you spend with them doing *Core 52* will be special for the rest of your lives.

Mark E. Moore, author of *Core 52*

Megan Howerton

WEEK 1

In the beginning, God created the heavens and the earth.

—GENESIS 1:1

LESSON TO LEARN

God created the heavens and the earth, and he invites us to create with him.

DAY 1

Look outside. Everything you see is part of God's creation. The sun, the clouds, the grass, the bugs—all part of creation. The very first sentence in the Bible tells us that God created the heavens and the earth.

Have you ever seen a house being built? It's nowhere near as big a job as creating the whole world, but it's still a big job! It takes a lot of people to make it happen. An architect designs the house. A builder builds the house. An engineer supplies light and water to the house. And then there's another role that most people don't think about: the homeowner. The homeowner decorates and takes care of the house. Creation works kind of the same way. God designed the world. Jesus made the world. The Spirit of God gives life to the people and animals. And we are the homeowners decorating and caring for the world.

God did a great job designing and building heaven and earth. But why did he do all that work? He created the world for the same reasons you create things. Think about all the ways you create. Maybe it's writing, painting, building Legos, or even finding new ways to fix your hair. Whatever it is that you're making, you're probably hoping that someone will enjoy it, compliment you, or be proud of you. Psalm 102:18 says, "Let this be recorded for a generation to come, so that a people yet to be created may praise the Lord." God created the world and everything in it so that all creation would praise him. And here's the cool part: creation didn't stop there. Creation never stops. God gave us the same desire to create and invites us to create along with him. God gave us the job of the homeowner. He wants us to continue to add creative touches to our world and take care of it. It's not complicated. Just create in the ways you enjoy. Write a song, invent a new dessert, paint a picture, or build with your hands. Then people can enjoy your creations just like we enjoy God's creation.

CHALLENGE

Create something (a song, a story, a treat, an art project—however you like to create), and share it with your family.

DAY 2

My job is to take care of the world and make the world better by creating with God.

MEMORY WORK

In the beginning, God created the heavens and the earth.
—GENESIS 1:1

DAY 3

READ GENESIS 1.

Imagine that you're watching God create the world. What does it look like? Sound like? Smell like?

What are some ways humans praise God? How do you think animals and plants praise him?

Why do you think God is compared to an architect, Jesus to a builder, and the Holy Spirit to an engineer?

DAY 4

READ GENESIS 2:1-22.

What did God provide that Adam and Eve needed? What has God provided for you?

How did Adam and Eve add to creation? How can you add to creation?

How do your parents provide for you like God provided for Adam and Eve?

DAY 5

MENTORING MOMENT

MENTOR "How does what you create bring praise to God?"

CHILD "How do you like to create? Were you always good at creating that way?"

MENTOR "How have you enjoyed someone else's creation recently?"

CHILD "How do you handle yourself when someone doesn't enjoy what you created?"

MENTOR "Are there things in creation that your friends might enjoy more than you do, such as sports, art, or music?"

CHILD "What's the difference between appreciating someone's creation and enjoying someone's creation?"

CHALLENGE CHECK

How did the challenge go? What did you learn?

WHO AM I?

God said, "Let us make human beings in our image."

—GENESIS 1:26, NLT

LESSON TO LEARN

Of all the things God ever made,
you are his favorite!

DAY 1

You've probably heard the saying "Save the best for last." We do this all the time. The best fireworks come at the end of the night. Dessert is at the end of a meal. Performers end a show with their most impressive act. That's exactly what God did when he created us. He saved the best for last. We are his favorite part of creation. In fact, God decided to create something in us that he didn't create in any other part of creation. He made humans in his own image. God put *his* qualities in us, things he didn't give to any plant or animal in all of creation.

God reveals himself to us through what he has made. We see the greatness of God when we look at the stars in the sky. We feel how big God is when we climb a mountain. We sense how powerful God is in the middle of a storm. But how can we experience God's patience, goodness, and love? These are qualities that we can't see—but we experience them through other people. Mom and Dad can demonstrate God's patience. A friend can show us God's goodness and love. And you can show others what God is like when you treat people like he does.

Another way we are like God is that we are creators. Everyone likes to make things. That's because God put his nature in us. We create things because he is creative. Humans are always making things and finding new ways to create. God gave us all different talents. You have talents that your friends probably don't have. You may even have talents that your parents don't have. God made you with special gifts. Some people create with their hands. Some create with words. Some create with pictures or music or cooking. This is God's creation at its finest. We were all created in God's image to be creators, but that doesn't mean that we create in the same ways. We are all special. And we all need the gifts others offer to make our world a special place.

CHALLENGE

Create something this week that would improve someone's day (cookies, a dance, a picture, a story . . .).

DAY 2

I am God's favorite part of creation. He put traits in me that are just like his traits, and I can use those to bring him glory.

MEMORY WORK

God said, "Let us make human beings in our image."
—GENESIS 1:26, NLT

DAY 3

READ EPHESIANS 1:1–14.

What's one of your strengths—something you like about yourself? Do you think God shares this trait? How?

What's a strength that someone else has that you don't have?

What's one of God's characteristics that you need to strengthen in yourself?

DAY 4

READ EPHESIANS 1:15–23.

Why do you think God loves the strength you identified yesterday? How can you use it to bring him glory?

Why is it important for different people to have different strengths? What would happen if we all had the same personality traits?

Since God blessed us all differently, why is it important to continue to strengthen our weaknesses?

DAY 5

MENTORING MOMENT

MENTOR "Do you know anyone else with the same gift? Do you use your gifts the same way?"

CHILD "How are you using your unique gifts?"

MENTOR "How do you think God will use your gifts when you're an adult?"

CHILD "How have your gifts grown as you have grown up?"

MENTOR "How do you feel about the gifts God has given you?"

CHILD "Have you ever wished God had given you different strengths? How did you still find value in the strengths he did give you?"

CHALLENGE CHECK

How did the challenge go? What did you learn?

WHAT IS MY PROBLEM?

When the woman saw that the fruit of the tree was good for food and pleasing to the eye, and also desirable for gaining wisdom, she took some and ate it. She also gave some to her husband, who was with her, and he ate it.

—GENESIS 3:6, NIV

LESSON TO LEARN

God puts parents, teachers, and other adults in our lives to protect us, not to ruin our fun.

Can you imagine living in the world right after God created it? You could have snuggled with a lion, surfed on a shark, and enjoyed a perfect world. Adam and Eve got to enjoy this ideal place. He just asked them to obey one command: "You must not eat fruit from the tree that is in the middle of the garden" (Genesis 3:3, NIV). Then one day Eve was tempted to eat fruit from this tree. She saw how beautiful it was. She imagined how delicious it was. And she thought it would make her wise. So she took a bite and gave some to Adam to eat too.

God wasn't concerned about the missing fruit. He was concerned about Adam's and Eve's hearts. That day something in their hearts changed forever. This one act of disobedience opened their eyes to see all the sin that they were capable of.

It's easy for us to read this story and see that God wanted only what was best for Adam and Eve. But when it's *our* story and temptation, it's not always as easy to see the clear choice. God wants to guide you to make good choices. Of course, we can always ask him to help, but he has also given us human helpers. And some of our greatest helpers are our parents. A toddler doesn't understand why her dad won't let her stick her finger in an electrical outlet. The toddler thinks it looks like fun, but the dad knows how dangerous it really is. The dad is only trying to do what's best for his child, but the baby thinks her fun has been ruined.

Now, think of a time when you thought your mom and dad were trying to ruin your fun. Maybe they wouldn't let you go to a friend's house. Maybe they stopped a wrestling match right when it was about to get really good. Parents aren't trying to ruin your fun. They are trying to keep you safe from dangers that you aren't aware of yet.

CHALLENGE

If you have been upset with someone who is only trying to protect you, ask for that person's forgiveness.

DAY 2

I make mistakes. But God has given me older and wiser people to help guide me.

MEMORY WORK

When the woman saw that the fruit of the tree was good for food and pleasing to the eye, and also desirable for gaining wisdom, she took some and ate it. She also gave some to her husband, who was with her, and he ate it.

—GENESIS 3:6, NIV

DAY 3

READ GENESIS 3:1–10.

 Can you remember a time when your mom and dad were trying to keep you safe but you thought your way was better?

 After Adam and Eve ate the fruit, how did they become more like God?

 Who or what in your life is most likely to tempt you to go against God's way?

DAY 4

READ GENESIS 4:1–16.

 If Adam and Eve hadn't sinned, do you think we would still be living in the Garden of Eden?

 How did Adam and Eve's choice to eat the fruit in the garden affect more lives than their own?

 How do your choices affect other people's lives?

DAY 5

MENTORING MOMENT

MENTOR "How do rules protect you?"

CHILD "Who has God given you to help you make wise decisions?"

MENTOR "How do boundaries and rules bring freedom?"

CHILD "Have you ever been saved from danger or pain by someone who was older and wiser than you?"

MENTOR "How do your actions reveal what's inside your heart?"

CHILD "Do you care more about my actions or about my heart (motivation)?"

CHALLENGE CHECK

How did the challenge go? What did you learn?

WEEK 4

HOW CAN I CONNECT WITH GOD?

[Abraham] believed the Lord, and he counted it to him as righteousness.

—GENESIS 15:6

LESSON TO LEARN

God always keeps his promises.

DAY 1

"I'll give you a turn—I promise!" "I'm telling the truth—I promise!" We've all said things like this. We've all heard things like this. A promise is supposed to mean real honesty, but unfortunately, sometimes people make promises they don't mean. But God always means it. When God makes a promise, he keeps it. He's so serious about keeping his promises that he even has a different word for them. God calls his promises "covenants."

One of the biggest covenants God made is in Genesis 12:2–3. He promised to bless Abraham's family and make his name great. Although this is a promise to Abraham, there is a promise in there for us too. God promised to bless all the families of the earth through Abraham. When we pray, we often thank God for the blessings he's given us—our homes, our friends, our health. These things are nice but are not what God was talking about. God promised Abraham the blessing of his Spirit. He promised that he would be with him even when things seemed impossible. He promised Abraham the blessing of his love, joy, and peace.

God kept his promise to Abraham. He gave him a son, who gave him grandchildren, who gave him great-grandchildren, and so on. Abraham's family was big! As Abraham's family grew, they didn't stay in one place. They traveled all over, sharing their knowledge of God with other people so that the whole world would have a chance to know the same great promise-keeping God that they knew.

As you learn more about Abraham, you'll learn that God required a lot from him. It wasn't an easy task keeping his end of the covenant and becoming the father of a great nation. Abraham kept God's covenant because he believed that God would keep his promise. If you want to be in this great family of God, he's going to have some expectations of you. It won't always be easy. But it will be blessed.

CHALLENGE

Write down your favorite promise from God. Put it somewhere you can see it, and read it every day (see day 3, level 1).

DAY 2

God gave us several ways to connect with him. One of those ways is the Bible and all its promises.

MEMORY WORK

[Abraham] believed the LORD, and he counted it to him as righteousness.
—GENESIS 15:6

DAY 3

READ GENESIS 21:1–7.

With help, look up these passages. What does God promise you in each of them?

- Matthew 11:28–29
- James 1:5
- Isaiah 41:13
- Philippians 4:6–9
- John 3:16

What's a promise God has made to you and kept?

What does it mean to you to be blessed? How is it similar to or different from God's promise to bless Abraham?

DAY 4

READ GENESIS 22:1–18.

Sometimes a covenant requires us to make sacrifices. What's something in your life that would be hard to give up if God asked you to?

How have you experienced God's blessing?

Is there a situation in your life where you don't feel like you can see God keeping his promises?

DAY 5

MENTORING MOMENT

MENTOR "What are some consequences of breaking a promise?"

CHILD "Have you ever had to make a sacrifice in order to keep a promise? How was that sacrifice worth it?"

MENTOR "What promise of God brings you the most comfort?"

CHILD "Tell me about a time when God kept a promise to you."

MENTOR "Do your friends see you as a promise keeper?"

CHILD "Did you ever break a promise, then regret breaking it?"

CHALLENGE CHECK

How did the challenge go?
What did you learn?

HOW DO I GET RIGHT WITH GOD?

I am the LORD who brought you up out of
the land of Egypt to be your God.
You shall therefore be holy, for I am holy.

—LEVITICUS 11:45

LESSON TO LEARN

You are holy because God says you are holy.

DAY 1

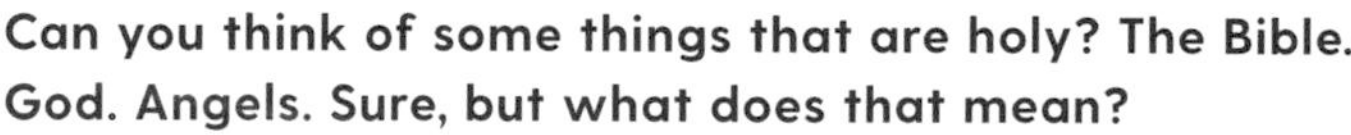

Can you think of some things that are holy? The Bible. God. Angels. Sure, but what does that mean?

Here is a riddle to explain it. What do you and your toothbrush have in common? You are both holy. It sounds crazy, but it's true. The word *holy* simply means "set apart." It's kind of like a wedding dress, which is used only for a special ceremony. Or your grandma's nice china, which is used only for special meals.

I know you aren't walking around telling your friends that you have a holy toothbrush, but you do show the holiness of your toothbrush by your actions. Toothbrushes could have lots of jobs. The most common job of a toothbrush is to brush teeth. But people also sometimes use a toothbrush to clean the toilet. Would you let your mom use *your* toothbrush to clean the toilet? Of course not! You set your toothbrush apart for the job of cleaning your teeth. It's okay for another toothbrush to be used to clean the toilet, but not *your* toothbrush! You see, your toothbrush is holy. What makes your toothbrush holy (or set apart)? It's not the toothbrush—it's you. It became holy when you claimed it as your own.

In the same way, you are holy because God says you are holy. Sometimes we try to be special to God by doing good things. News flash: You can't be good enough to earn holiness. But you already have God's attention and his love. He is crazy about you. You don't become holy by reading your Bible every day or by doing all your chores. You are holy because God chose you to be his child. It's one of his many gifts to us. We do good things because we are thankful for his gifts, not because we have to earn them.

CHALLENGE

Look at yourself in the mirror every morning, and say to yourself, "I am holy because God says I am holy."

DAY 2

Holiness can't be earned. You are holy because God says you are holy.

MEMORY WORK

I am the Lord who brought you up out of the land of Egypt to be your God. You shall therefore be holy, for I am holy.
—LEVITICUS 11:45

DAY 3

READ 1 PETER 2:9–10.

What makes you part of your family?

When you disobey your parents, you don't suddenly stop being part of the family. But what does happen?

Have you ever tried to earn holiness? How?

DAY 4

READ PSALM 51:1–12.

David is desperate for forgiveness and holiness in this psalm. What does it feel like to be desperate for forgiveness?

What verse in this psalm do you relate to most?

David's plea for forgiveness doesn't pass blame or make excuses. Why is that important?

DAY 5

MENTORING MOMENT

MENTOR "What are some similarities between being part of our family and being part of the family of God?"

CHILD "How am I holy (set apart, special, chosen) in this family?"

MENTOR "If you viewed your friends like God does, would it change the way you treat them? What about your enemies?"

CHILD "How did your heart change when you realized you can't earn holiness?"

MENTOR "What's the difference between being holy and being good?"

CHILD "God calls me holy. What should I do because of it?"

CHALLENGE CHECK

How did the challenge go? What did you learn?

WEEK 6

IS JESUS AS GOOD AS THEY SAY?

I will raise up for them a prophet like you from among their brothers. And I will put my words in his mouth, and he shall speak to them all that I command him.

—DEUTERONOMY 18:18

LESSON TO LEARN

Jesus is the savior of the world. But he chooses imperfect people to do his work.

DAY 1

On June 20, 1936, Jesse Owens became the world's fastest man. He held that title for twenty years. Then, on August 3, 1956, Willie Williams beat his time and became the new fastest man in the world. In fact, since Jesse Owens, there have been several new world records and world-record holders.

Moses was the most important leader of Israel. He was kind of like George Washington or Abraham Lincoln in the United States. When he was a baby, he was adopted by the princess of Egypt. He grew up in the palace while his people served the pharaoh as slaves. Then God called Moses to rescue his people, the Israelites, from slavery. It's easy to see how Moses was such a hero to the Israelites. He saved them. They owed him everything.

Jesus is the Son of God, raised by a woman named Mary. He was sent from heaven to earth to teach us about God. He ultimately showed us the great love God has for us by dying on the cross for the forgiveness of our sins. He didn't stay dead, though. He rose again, beating death, so that we could live with him forever.

Moses saved his people from slavery. Jesus saves the world from sin and death. Before Jesus came to earth, many people thought that Moses was the greatest. Moses *was* the greatest in the same way that Jesse Owens *was* the fastest man in the world. Just like Jesse Owens is still thought of as a great athlete, Moses is still considered a great Israelite hero. But Jesus is the ultimate savior of the world, and only he can be the greatest.

CHALLENGE

Mentor, assign your child a task you know they will need your help with. Do this to model how God always gives us the help we need to do what he asks us to do.

DAY 2

Jesus is the savior of the world. No one can replace him, but we can be his hands and feet, doing his work in this world.

MEMORY WORK

I will raise up for them a prophet like you from among their brothers. And I will put my words in his mouth, and he shall speak to them all that I command him.
—DEUTERONOMY 18:18

DAY 3

READ EXODUS 2:11–15 AND EXODUS 3:1–12.

Does God want to use you even after you've made a mistake? How?

How is it more impressive when God uses someone who isn't qualified?

Are you ever really qualified to do God's work? What makes it possible?

DAY 4

READ EXODUS 4:10–17.

What excuse did Moses give God for why he didn't think he'd be able to complete the task? What was God's response?

Have you ever felt disqualified from doing God's work because of past mistakes?

What are the reasons you think you can't do what God asks of you?

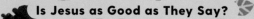

DAY 5

MENTORING MOMENT

MENTOR "When I'm disappointed in you, do you still feel like I believe in you?"

CHILD "Does God still believe in us even when we disappoint him?"

MENTOR "What do you think God is asking you to do right now?"

CHILD "Has God helped you do something even when you didn't think you could?"

MENTOR "How can I encourage or help you in doing what God has asked you to do?"

CHILD "Have you ever not done what God wanted you to do? What happened?"

CHALLENGE CHECK

How did the challenge go?
What did you learn?

WEEK 7

WHAT IS GOD LOOKING FOR IN LEADERS?

Do not look on his appearance or on the height of his stature, because I have rejected him. For the LORD sees not as man sees: man looks on the outward appearance, but the LORD looks on the heart.

—1 SAMUEL 16:7

LESSON TO LEARN

God's plan is always best.

DAY 1

If your parent's smartphone were to break, would they take it to a car mechanic to have it fixed? Of course not. That would be silly. The mechanic didn't invent or build the phone. They would take it to a phone store, where the employees have the tools and ability to fix the phone so it could work in the way it was intended to work.

In the same way, God designed his creation. His plan is the best plan for how things should work. When creation goes along with God's plan, things run smoothly. Most of creation goes along with God's perfect plan. The sun rises and sets every day. The rain makes the plants grow. The plants provide food for animals, and sometimes those animals are food for other animals. But do you know what things don't always work the way God made them? You and me! God gave us the ability to make our own decisions. That is wonderful. But sometimes we make decisions that go against God's plan.

This is what was happening in Israel in our Bible reading this week. God's plan was to be the king of the Israelites. They didn't need a human ruler. But the people thought that they knew better. They wanted a human king. So that's what they got. A man named Saul became their king. The Israelites thought that Saul would be a good king. He had the qualities that they thought a good king should have—he was rich, handsome, and strong. But Saul ended up not being the best man for the job because he didn't have the right kind of heart.

We can be like the Israelites sometimes. We decide to make our own plan, find our own king, and throw God's plan out the window. Our king isn't a man named Saul. We might have many kings, and they all go by different names: entertainment, favorite brands, sports, friends, popularity. Sometimes we don't even realize these things are replacing God as the king of our hearts. None of these things are bad, but when we treat them as more important than God, we stray from the plan that God has for us. And God's plan is always best.

CHALLENGE

Identify one thing you usually do with the wrong attitude. This week, complete the task with a happy heart.

DAY 2

God wants leaders who will point people to him, our true leader.

MEMORY WORK

Do not look on his appearance or on the height of his stature, because I have rejected him. For the LORD sees not as man sees: man looks on the outward appearance, but the LORD looks on the heart.
—1 SAMUEL 16:7

DAY 3

READ 1 SAMUEL 15:20–23.

Why did God reject Saul as king?

What's the difference between the character traits that are important to the world and what's important to God?

It's possible to do the right action with the wrong attitude. What's something you do that you need to change your attitude about?

DAY 4

READ 1 SAMUEL 16:6–7.

Why does God care more about the heart than the outward appearance?

What words would you want someone to use to describe your heart?

What can you do to practice having the kind of heart that you want?

DAY 5

MENTORING MOMENT

MENTOR "What are you prioritizing: outward appearance or the heart?"

CHILD "How are your character traits pointing people to Jesus?"

MENTOR "Are there any character traits you're known for that you want to change?"

CHILD "Have you ever had to work on any character traits? How did you do it?"

MENTOR "What kind of heart does God want leaders to have?"

CHILD "Saul had blind spots in obeying the LORD. What are my blind spots that could keep me from being a leader?"

CHALLENGE CHECK

How did the challenge go? What did you learn?

WEEK 8

DOES GOD DIRECT HISTORY?

When your days are over and you rest with your ancestors, I will raise up your offspring to succeed you, your own flesh and blood, and I will establish his kingdom.

—2 SAMUEL 7:12, NIV

LESSON TO LEARN

Jesus came to be king of your heart.

DAY 1

Have you ever taken a big drink of water only to find out that it was actually Sprite? Wow! Even if you love it, getting a mouthful of Sprite when you expected to get a mouthful of water is really shocking. That can happen a lot in life. Things don't always turn out the way we expect. And that can be hard to adjust to.

Before Jesus came to earth, people thought they knew what he would look like, act like, and be like. In 2 Samuel 7:12, God promised that there would be an heir to the throne of King David. Many Jews expected an earthly king to show up: a guy with money, power, and a big army. But Jesus was a carpenter. He didn't have money. He didn't have power or an army. He just had a few followers and a great big dream. How could he possibly protect the nation of Israel and lead them to greatness?

But Jesus never wanted to rule only Israel. He saw a bigger picture. He saw each Israelite, and he also saw each person that wasn't an Israelite. He saw you and me in the future too. His kingdom was unexpected but so much greater than anyone thought it would be. Jesus's kingdom starts with his being king of our lives. Jesus came to be king of your heart, not of a country. He wants to rule with love, not with force. He wants to lead people with truth, not with power or popularity. He wants everyone to be part of his kingdom. And being part of his kingdom is better than anything anyone could ever imagine.

CHALLENGE

Give up one thing that you really love this week. Every time you think about that thing, ask for God's help in making him king of your heart.

DAY 2

Sometimes God does things differently than we expect, but he has a plan, and part of that plan is to be king of your heart.

MEMORY WORK

I will raise up your offspring to succeed you, your own flesh and blood, and I will establish his kingdom.
—2 SAMUEL 7:12, NIV

DAY 3

READ MATTHEW 21:6–11.

Who is the most important person you've ever met? How did you treat that person?

Jesus was, by earthly standards, an ordinary man entering Jerusalem like a king. If you had been in the crowd that day, what do you think you would have thought and felt?

Why did people expect Jesus to be different than he was?

DAY 4

READ MATTHEW 22:15–22.

Jesus said to give God what belongs to him. How can we do that?

What's something that you're holding on to that should belong to God?

Why is it so hard to give God everything?

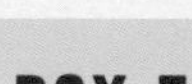

DAY 5

MENTORING MOMENT

MENTOR "When someone makes Jesus king of their heart, how does their life begin to look different?"

CHILD "What's something I'm holding on to that I need to give to God?"

MENTOR "Do you have expectations about how you think God should treat you?"

CHILD "Will my unmet expectations make more sense the older I get?"

MENTOR "Have you ever felt like God wasn't meeting your expectations?"

CHILD "What do you do when you feel like God isn't meeting your expectations?"

CHALLENGE CHECK

How did the challenge go? What did you learn?

WEEK 9

HOW CAN I FIND HAPPINESS?

Happy is the person who
doesn't listen to the wicked.
He doesn't go where sinners go.
He doesn't do what bad people do.
He loves the Lord's teachings.
He thinks about those
teachings day and night.
He is strong, like a tree planted
by a river.
It produces fruit in season.
Its leaves don't die.
Everything he does will succeed.

—PSALM 1:1–3, ICB

LESSON TO LEARN

God cares about your happiness.

DAY 1

Do your mom and dad want you to be happy? Can you think of anything they do to help you be happy? You know what? That's just like God. He wants you to be happy too. Some people may feel that God *doesn't* want them to be happy. Maybe you've heard people say that God cares only how good you are, not how happy you are. But understanding how our parents want us to be happy helps us understand how God wants us to be happy.

Sometimes it may seem like your parents don't want you to be happy. They do! But they want you to be happy for a long time, not just right now. For example, they want you to be safe. So they may not let you ride a skateboard in the middle of the street, because they know better than you what could happen. Or your dad wants you to have a good attitude and be able to focus on school tomorrow so you can enjoy time with your classmates and learn what you need to learn. That's why he told you to turn off the video game. He knows how grumpy and groggy you get without enough sleep. When it feels like your parents are fighting against your happiness, they are probably really fighting against something *now* that will damage your happiness long term.

Just like your parents want you to be happy, God also wants you to be happy. Sometimes life gets hard. Maybe you're having a hard time keeping your grades up, your parents got divorced, or you didn't get invited to a party. Do sad situations mean that God doesn't want you to be happy? Of course not! Look around. Opportunities for happiness are everywhere. God gave us mountains to climb, music to listen to, and people to love. Instead, let's ask, "In this situation, how could God be protecting me and preparing for my future happiness?" You may not always be able to answer that question, but when hard times come, you can always trust that God is caring for your long-term happiness rather than your immediate happiness.

CHALLENGE

Think about a rule your parents have that you don't understand. Ask them how that rule is for your long-term happiness.

Asking God to be the king of your life will naturally bring happiness, but it's *not* a promise that nothing bad will ever happen to you. Sometimes it's the hard times that help us remember that we need God to be the king of our lives. Look at Job. He had to endure some terrible losses. But those difficulties drew him closer to God. He used his hardships to show the world that he trusted God to care for his long-term happiness.

DAY 2

God cares about your happiness. That's why he has given you boundaries. Happiness is found within the boundaries God has designed for us.

MEMORY WORK

Happy is the person who doesn't listen to the wicked.
He doesn't go where sinners go.
He doesn't do what bad people do.
He loves the LORD's teachings.
He thinks about those teachings day and night.
—PSALM 1:1–2, ICB

DAY 3

READ JOB 1:6–22.

What was Job's reaction to the news of all he had lost?

Have you ever had a big loss? How did you respond?

What do our reactions to difficult situations reveal about our hearts?

DAY 4

READ JOB 2:7–13.

Who would encourage you in hard times?

Why is it important to have people who are there for you?

What's the difference between long- and short-term happiness?

DAY 5

MENTORING MOMENT

MENTOR "Do you know anyone going through a hard time right now? How can you be there for them?"

CHILD "Is it okay to be sad sometimes?"

MENTOR "Do you feel like you need God more in hard times or when things are good? Why?"

CHILD "Tell me about a time when you felt like you needed God."

MENTOR "What can you do right now to prepare for hard times ahead?"

CHILD "When do you see me focusing on short-term happiness over long-term happiness?"

CHALLENGE CHECK

How did the challenge go? What did you learn?

WEEK 10

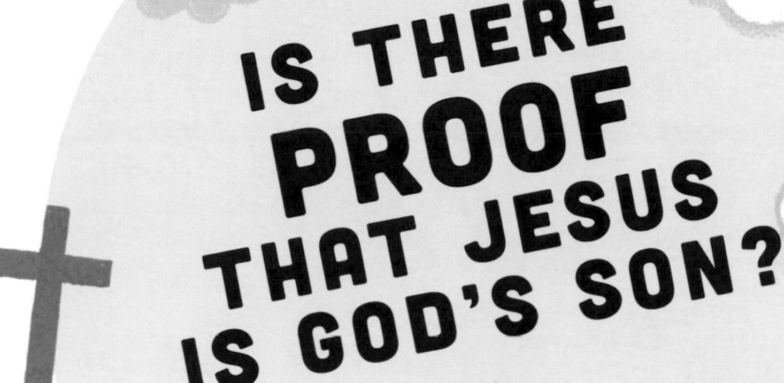

IS THERE PROOF THAT JESUS IS GOD'S SON?

You are my son;
today I have become your father.

—PSALM 2:7, NIV

LESSON TO LEARN

God's plan is intentional.

DAY 1

Pretend you have a cup full of one hundred pennies. You paint one penny red, mix it in with the others, and randomly pick one penny from the cup. Your chances of grabbing the painted penny are one in one hundred. It's possible to pick the painted penny randomly, but if someone were to pick the penny on their first draw, you would probably think they were peeking. What if, instead of a cup, you had a pickup truck full of pennies? What would the chances be then?

The Bible is full of promises called prophecies. *Prophecy* is a fancy word for "prediction." You may have even heard that Jesus fulfilled prophecies. He did! There are more than sixty major prophecies about Jesus. They predicted things like where he would be born (Micah 5:2), that he would enter Jerusalem riding on a donkey (Zechariah 9:9), and that he would be crucified (Psalm 22:16). The chance of one person fulfilling just seven of these sixty prophecies is one in one hundred quadrillion—that's 100,000,000,000,000,000. Whoa! Can you even count that high? After hundreds comes thousands, then millions, billions, trillions, and *then* quadrillions.

Jesus fulfilled all sixty prophecies. This means there was nothing random about it. Nothing was left to chance. God didn't want us to have to wonder whether Jesus was the Messiah. He wasn't blindfolded, trying to pick a painted penny. He had a plan. He made it abundantly clear that Jesus, his Son, was the Messiah sent to save the world. It couldn't have happened by accident. Jesus was a specific person sent to a specific place at a specific time in history to complete a specific task.

CHALLENGE

Every night this week, lay out your clothes for the next day as a reminder that God's plan was in place before you were born.

DAY 2

Jesus fulfilled prophecies, proving that God's plan was intentional.

MEMORY WORK

You are my son; today I have become your father.

—PSALM 2:7, NIV

DAY 3

READ PSALM 22:1–24.

Use the chart to compare the prophecies in Psalm 22 to the fulfillment of the prophecies in the New Testament. As a family, discuss what prophecies were fulfilled. Use the first row as an example.

VERSE	PROPHECY	PROPHECY FULFILLED IN NEW TESTAMENT
22:1–21	Jesus will go through physical and emotional pain on the cross.	Matthew 27:31
22:15	WHAT DO YOU THINK THE PROPHECY COULD BE?	John 19:28 (NIV) "Knowing that everything had now been finished, and so that Scripture would be fulfilled, Jesus said, 'I am thirsty.'"
22:18	WHAT DO YOU THINK THE PROPHECY COULD BE?	John 19:23–24 (NIV) "When the soldiers crucified Jesus, they took his clothes, dividing them into four shares, one for each of them, with the undergarment remaining. This garment was seamless, woven in one piece from top to bottom. 'Let's not tear it,' they said to one another. 'Let's decide by lot who will get it.'"
22:16	WHAT DO YOU THINK THE PROPHECY COULD BE?	John 19:18 "There they crucified him, and with him two others, one on either side, and Jesus between them."

Match Acts 4:11 and Matthew 21:9 from the New Testament to the prophecies they fulfill in Psalm 118, verses 22 and 26.

Match Acts 4:25–26; Matthew 3:17; and Revelation 12:5 from the New Testament to the prophecies they fulfill in Psalm 2, verses 1–2, 7, and 9.

DAY 4

READ REVELATION 19:11–16.

What is this prophecy talking about?

Why is this prophecy important?

What does God want Christians to do because of this prophecy?

DAY 5

MENTORING MOMENT

MENTOR "What was the hardest prophecy for Jesus to fulfill?"

CHILD "Why was it hard to fulfill these prophecies?"

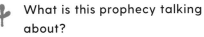

MENTOR "How can we be more intentional with God?"

CHILD "Have you lived more intentionally at times?"

MENTOR "What do you think God's plan is for you today?"

CHILD "How does it make you proud when I live out God's plan for me?"

CHALLENGE CHECK

How did the challenge go?
What did you learn?

IS GOD
REALLY
WATCHING OUT
FOR ME?

The LORD is my shepherd; I shall not want.
He makes me lie down in green pastures.
He leads me beside still waters.
He restores my soul.

—PSALM 23:1–3

LESSON TO LEARN

Jesus cares for you like a good shepherd cares for his sheep.

DAY 1

Can you finish this nursery rhyme? "Mary had a little . . ." What about this Bible verse? "The LORD is my . . ." That is Psalm 23:1. Why did God say that he is your shepherd? Because he wants to take care of you like a shepherd takes care of his sheep. A good shepherd makes sure his sheep have food, water, and protection. If the sheep obey their good shepherd, everything should run smoothly. Why does the Bible need to mention that Jesus is the *good* shepherd (John 10:11)? It would be a beautiful thing if all shepherds were good, but unfortunately, not all shepherds are. Some shepherds don't protect their sheep. But Jesus always protects you. He always has your best interests in mind.

People are a lot like sheep. We need to eat, drink, and be kept safe. We also have spiritual needs. We're hungry for biblical truth, thirsty for a relationship with our Creator, and in need of godly wisdom to help us with difficult situations that could be dangerous for our hearts and souls. Whether we realize it or not, we turn to shepherds to guide us. When we're very young, our parents and other trusted adults are our shepherds. As we get older, we start to choose our own shepherds. But sometimes we don't follow the Good Shepherd. Maybe you're looking to a sport, popularity, or a friend to guide you. Having godly friends and adults that help guide us is important, and I hope you have them. But they can't replace Jesus as your shepherd. When sheep don't follow their shepherd, they end up hungry, thirsty, or in danger. When we follow anything besides the Good Shepherd, we end up with unmet spiritual needs. We will be thirsty for a relationship with our Creator, hungry for biblical truth in our lives, and lacking the wisdom to handle tricky situations. No person or thing will ever meet your needs better than Jesus, the Good Shepherd.

CHALLENGE

Make a list of what it takes to care for a dog, cat, hamster, bird, or fish. Then ask your mentor what they would add to the list.

DAY 2

Jesus cares for you like a good shepherd cares for his sheep, and your spiritual health is most important to him.

MEMORY WORK

The Lord is my shepherd; I shall not want.
He makes me lie down in green pastures.
He leads me beside still waters.
He restores my soul.
—PSALM 23:1–3

DAY 3

REPHRASE PSALM 23 IN YOUR OWN WORDS:

The Lord is my shepherd; I shall not want.
Example: *I follow Jesus. I don't need any other person or thing to be the ultimate guide of my life.*
He makes me lie down in green pastures.
He leads me beside still waters.
He restores my soul.
He leads me in paths of righteousness
for his name's sake.

Even though I walk through the valley of the shadow of death,
I will fear no evil,
for you are with me;
your rod and your staff,
they comfort me.

You prepare a table before me
in the presence of my enemies;
you anoint my head with oil;
my cup overflows.
Surely goodness and mercy shall follow me
all the days of my life,
and I shall dwell in the house of the Lord forever.

Which of these verses makes you feel most protected by Jesus?

Based on these verses, in what ways do you need to trust Jesus more?

What can you do to improve your spiritual health?

DAY 4

READ JOHN 10:1–18.

What does Jesus do for you that a shepherd does for his sheep?

How can you recognize Jesus's voice even though you can't hear it out loud?

How does the thief try to break into your life?

MENTOR "What other voices try to get your attention?"

CHILD "What are my biggest distractions that could keep me from following the voice of Jesus?"

MENTOR "What safeguards would help you ignore other voices so you can listen to Jesus's voice?"

CHILD "How have you learned to follow Jesus more closely?"

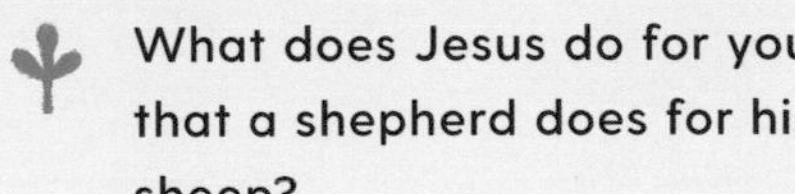

DAY 5

MENTORING MOMENT

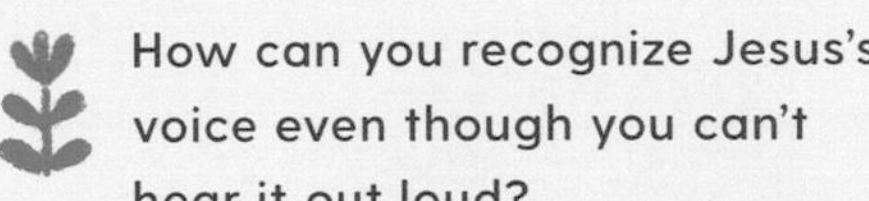

MENTOR "How have you felt cared for by Jesus lately?"

CHILD "How is the way you protect me like how Jesus protects me? How is it different?"

CHALLENGE CHECK

How did the challenge go? What did you learn?

WEEK 12

The LORD says to my Lord:
"Sit at my right hand,
until I make your enemies your footstool."

—PSALM 110:1

LESSON TO LEARN

Jesus is our savior.

DAY 1 *"I believe Jesus is the Christ, the Son of the living God."*

People say these words when they are baptized. This statement comes from Matthew 16:16. Jesus had just asked his disciples, "Who do you say that I am?" (verse 15). These disciples got to travel around with Jesus. They saw great miracles and heard great teachings. They all believed that Jesus was a great prophet, but for the first time, one of Jesus's disciples finally understood that Jesus was the promised king, the heir to David's throne. The Jews called that king "Messiah." As Christians, we believe that too. Jesus is our king and savior. When we are baptized, we show with our actions (baptism) and our words (confession of faith) that Jesus is our savior. Such an important statement deserves a very clear explanation.

I believe What does your mom mean when she says, "I believe in you"? She thinks you can overcome whatever challenge is in front of you. Maybe it's a sport, a musical instrument, or your homework. In the same way, we say to Jesus, "I believe." We believe he is powerful enough to lead our lives.

Jesus is the Christ Did you know that the Bible wasn't written in English? Most of the Old Testament was written in Hebrew, and most of the New Testament was written in Greek. In the Old Testament, we see the word *Messiah*. In the New Testament, the word *Christ* is more common. It's the same word—*Christ* is the Greek word for "Messiah." They both mean "anointed one." Jesus is often referred to as Jesus Christ or sometimes just Christ. It's similar to us using the term *doctor* or *officer* when we refer to someone in one of those positions. When *Christ* appears after Jesus's name, it simply means "Jesus, the anointed one." Whether you say it in Hebrew, Greek, or English, if you believe that Jesus is the Christ, you believe that he was chosen by God to save the world.

The Son of the living God Have people ever told you, "You look just like your mom"? Or "You have your father's eyes"? We all resemble our parents in some way. Since Jesus lived before cameras were invented, we don't really know what he looked like. But we do know that he had

the heart of his Father. He acted like God does. He died for the sins of the world so that anyone who wanted to chase after the heart of the Father could live with him forever in heaven. He did all that because of his love for us. He loves you that much! And he loves your neighbor that much. We also get to call God our Father. We might have our dads' eyes or smile. But God wants us to have his heart.

CHALLENGE

Ask three people to tell you the first character trait they think of when they think of you. Compare those traits with the heart of the Father.

DAY 2

Jesus came to be the savior of the world. We all have a choice whether to accept him as our savior.

MEMORY WORK

The LORD says to my Lord:
"Sit at my right hand,
until I make your enemies your footstool."
—PSALM 110:1

DAY 3

READ JOHN 5:19–29.

How does someone get eternal life (verse 24)?

What makes Jesus a savior?

How can you show Jesus that you want him to be your savior?

DAY 4

READ JOHN 6:41-59.

What do you imagine eternal life will be like?

What are the two kinds of bread Jesus was talking about (verses 48–51)?

What things do you think stop people from making Jesus their savior?

DAY 5

MENTORING MOMENT

MENTOR "Do you have any questions about who Jesus is?"

CHILD "Have you ever questioned your faith?"

MENTOR "What do you believe about Jesus?"

CHILD "When did you know you believed in Jesus?"

MENTOR "What does it mean to have the heart of the Father?"

CHILD "What does a person need to know before getting baptized?"

CHALLENGE CHECK

How did the challenge go?
What did you learn?

WEEK 13

IF JESUS WAS REJECTED, WHY SHOULD I ACCEPT HIM?

The stone that the builders rejected
has become the cornerstone.

—PSALM 118:22

LESSON TO LEARN

Jesus is the only foundation solid enough to build your life on.

DAY 1

If you wanted to build the tallest Lego tower ever, how would you begin? Most likely you would want to make sure your tower had a strong base or foundation. Without a strong foundation, the tower wouldn't last long before falling over. In Psalm 118:22, the word *cornerstone* means "foundation." And that foundation, it turns out, is Jesus. Jesus spent years trying to tell people, including his disciples, exactly who he was. After his death and resurrection, many people recognized him as the Messiah, or king. They saw him as the strong base that they could build the rest of their faith on. Although many people had this view, there were still people who rejected him. Why? Maybe they rejected Jesus because he didn't meet their expectations. Maybe it was because they thought he wasn't really who he claimed to be. Maybe it was because they just didn't like his teachings or they weren't ready to put God first in their lives. Whatever the reasons were, the people who rejected Jesus didn't have a strong foundation.

People still reject Jesus today and choose not to have him as their foundation. When Jesus is your foundation, he will be able to comfort you when you're sad, help you control your temper when you're angry, and help you show love to people even when they aren't very loving. If your foundation is anything other than Jesus, it will crumble under pressure.

So, how can you make sure your foundation is Jesus? Spend time getting to know him. Pray. Study the Bible. The Bible says that God is unchanging. The God of the Bible is the same God we serve. We can learn a lot about him just by reading our Bibles. He wants to reveal his heart to you if you seek to know it.

CHALLENGE

Spend five to ten minutes reading your Bible and praying every day this week.

DAY 2

The truth about Jesus doesn't depend on whether he was accepted. But your faith does depend on your foundation. Jesus is the only foundation solid enough to build your life on.

MEMORY WORK

The stone that the builders rejected
has become the cornerstone.
—PSALM 118:22

DAY 3

READ ACTS 4:1–4.

Why were the Jewish leaders upset with Peter and John?

How would you respond if someone reacted badly because you talked about Jesus or invited them to church? Has this ever happened?

What would you be willing to lose for sharing Jesus with others?

DAY 4

READ ACTS 4:5–22.

If you knew you would be insulted or hurt for talking about Jesus, how would you prepare?

The Jewish leaders could tell that Peter and John had been with Jesus. How can people tell that you've spent time with Jesus?

Why were some religious leaders so afraid of Jesus's name being spread? Do you think people are still afraid of that today?

DAY 5

MENTORING MOMENT

MENTOR "What are some things you could do to make sure Jesus is the foundation of your life?"

CHILD "Have you ever suffered because you're a Christian?"

MENTOR "Will making Jesus your foundation make your life easy? Explain."

CHILD "Why do you want Jesus to be your foundation?"

MENTOR "Do you have any fears about sharing Jesus with people?"

CHILD "How did your life change when you made Jesus your foundation?"

CHALLENGE CHECK

How did the challenge go? What did you learn?

WEEK 14

The fear of the Lord is the beginning of knowledge; fools despise wisdom and instruction.

—PROVERBS 1:7

LESSON TO LEARN

Wisdom is a treasure. Go get it!

DAY 1

Proverbs 1:7 says, "The fear of the LORD is the beginning of knowledge." This idea is found again in Proverbs 9:10 and 15:33 with the word *wisdom* used instead of *knowledge*. The important words to understand in these verses are *fear* and *wisdom*. We usually associate fear with negative feelings and wisdom with positive feelings. How can something bad be the beginning of something good?

It's quite simple, actually. Fear isn't always bad. Let's use fire as an example. Most people fear fire. Most of us don't spend much time and energy thinking about fire. It doesn't cause us to have anxious thoughts. But the fear of fire causes us to respect it. People tend to a fire and make sure they follow safety rules when using fire because they understand how powerful it can be. Parents keep a closer watch on their children near fire. You often have to get permission to have a fire in your backyard. People even blow out the tiny flames of candles before going to bed or leaving their house because of the respect they have for fire.

Sometimes we fear things like monsters under our bed. That kind of fear doesn't protect us or help us in any way. Your fear of God should resemble the fear of fire, not the fear of monsters under your bed. Just like fearing fire can help keep you safe, so can fearing God. When you fear God, you're recognizing his power and greatness. Fear of God comes from respect for his power. These Bible verses are all saying that we can get wisdom by fearing the Lord. It can be tricky to choose wisdom when life is actually happening to you. Here are a few examples:

CHALLENGE

Pray for wisdom every day this week. At the end of the week, give one example of how God answered your prayer.

SITUATION	FOOLISHNESS SAYS . . .	WISDOM SAYS . . .
YOUR SISTER TOOK SOMETHING FROM YOUR ROOM WITHOUT ASKING.	Grab it from her hands and yell, "You aren't allowed in my room!"	Ask for it back with gentleness.
YOU'RE AT A FRIEND'S HOUSE AND YOUR FRIEND IS WATCHING A SHOW YOUR PARENTS WOULDN'T ALLOW.	Go along with it. Your parents won't find out anyway.	Explain that you aren't allowed to watch that show, and ask to switch to something else.
A CLASSMATE IS BEING TEASED ABOUT HIS SHIRT.	Do nothing, and be glad you're not the one getting teased. Or participate in the teasing. It is a pretty terrible shirt.	Stand up for your classmate, and treat him how you would want to be treated in that situation.

When we fear God, we understand that his ways are always best. His ways aren't a secret. James 1:5 promises, "If any of you lacks wisdom, you should ask God, who gives generously to all without finding fault, and it will be given to you" (NIV). What great news! God wants us to have *his* wisdom—we just need to ask for it. That doesn't mean that we will never make a foolish choice again. But as we grow in our respect for God and make a habit of asking for his wisdom, we will find that happens less and less.

DAY 2

An appropriate fear of God is the beginning of wisdom.

MEMORY WORK

The fear of the Lord is the beginning of knowledge;
fools despise wisdom and instruction.
—PROVERBS 1:7

DAY 3

READ 1 KINGS 3:5–15.

God gave Solomon the wisdom he asked for. If God told you he would give you anything you wanted, what would you ask for?

Why would fools despise wisdom?

Why do you think God blessed Solomon with both wisdom and wealth?

DAY 4

READ 1 KINGS 11:1–13.

What consequences did Solomon face for turning away from God?

What could be some consequences in your life if you don't seek and follow God's wisdom?

How might Solomon's life have been different had he continued asking God for wisdom?

DAY 5

MENTORING MOMENT

MENTOR "Have you ever made a foolish decision? What consequences did that have?"

CHILD "How have you grown in wisdom?"

MENTOR "What's a situation you're facing where you need God's wisdom?"

CHILD "How can I make sure not to waste the gifts God has given me?"

MENTOR "Some of the consequences for Solomon's choices were immediate, and some were delayed. What could some delayed consequences be for your choices?"

CHILD "Do you have any lasting consequences from poor choices?"

CHALLENGE CHECK

How did the challenge go?
What did you learn?

WEEK 15

HOW CAN JESUS'S DEATH TAKE CARE OF MY PROBLEMS?

He was pierced for our transgressions,
he was crushed for our iniquities;
the punishment that brought us peace was on him,
and by his wounds we are healed.

—ISAIAH 53:5, NIV

LESSON TO LEARN

Jesus gave his life for our sins so that we can live.

DAY 1

Have you seen people take communion at church? It sounds a little weird, doesn't it? "This is my blood. Drink it to remember me." ***What?*** **Drink blood? For the record, Jesus never asked anyone to drink real blood. He shared wine with his disciples at the Last Supper, and most churches today use wine or grape juice as a symbol of Jesus's blood and bread as a symbol of Jesus's body. But what does it all actually mean? Let's go back to the very beginning.**

Think back to the Garden of Eden. After they ate the fruit, Adam and Eve realized that they were naked, and God clothed them with "garments of skins" (Genesis 3:21). Romans 6:23 says, "The wages of sin is death." In the Old Testament, sacrificing an animal was a way for that animal to take your place. Adam and Eve were literally wearing the skin of an animal that gave its life to save theirs. They were covered by the sacrifice of the animal. To put it another way, the animal's sacrifice atoned for Adam and Eve's sins. *Atonement* means that your sins have been covered or taken care of.

But that animal had to be perfect, "a male without blemish" or imperfections (Leviticus 1:3). Already we can see the similarities to the sacrifice of Jesus. He was the sinless Son who gave his life to pay for our sins. Jesus made atonement for our sins by dying in our place.

Often lambs were used as sacrifices. That's why Jesus is sometimes referred to as the Lamb of God. And we still hear statements like "We are covered by his blood," much like Adam and Eve were covered by the sacrifice of the animal. The difference is that Jesus's sacrifice wasn't temporary. His sacrifice lasts forever because he is the perfect sacrifice. He took our punishment. And now we can be forgiven.

So, next time you hear this weird blood-drinking talk, remember that it's just a symbol of the sacrifice Jesus made so that we could be free from the guilt of our sin and live in heaven for eternity.

CHALLENGE

If you disobey your parents this week, ask them for forgiveness and ask God for forgiveness (1 John 1:9).

DAY 2

Problems began when sin entered the world. Jesus was the ultimate sacrifice for everyone in the world to experience forgiveness.

MEMORY WORK

He was pierced for our transgressions,
he was crushed for our iniquities;
the punishment that brought us peace was on him,
and by his wounds we are healed.
—ISAIAH 53:5, NIV

DAY 3

READ EXODUS 7:14–8:32.

 Why do you think Pharaoh had a hard heart?

 What does it look like for a person to have a hard heart?

 Why is Jesus's sacrifice necessary for all of us?

DAY 4

READ EXODUS 11.

The pattern from Exodus 7–8 continued in Exodus 9–10. Pharaoh was sinful, decided he would change, and then went back to his wicked ways. His heart was still hard after nine plagues. It took the serious consequence of the death of the firstborn sons before Pharaoh would obey the commands of God.

 Have you ever disobeyed your parents? What were the consequences? How is that like the story of Pharaoh?

 Hiding your sins won't make them disappear. How can you fight your patterns of sin?

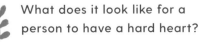

 God gave up his Son for your sins to be forgiven. What do you need to give up to live a life more pleasing to him?

DAY 5

Good news! Jesus died for your sins. He died for the ones you have a pattern of doing. He died for the ones you didn't mean to do. He even died for the ones you haven't done yet.

MENTORING MOMENT

MENTOR "How hard do you think it was for God to give up his Son for our sins?"

CHILD "When you give me a consequence, what do you hope will happen?"

MENTOR "How are you disobeying God when you disobey your parents?"

CHILD "If I don't want to sin, why do I continue to do it?"

MENTOR "If God doesn't expect perfection, what does he expect?"

CHILD "How is the way you want me to behave similar to the way God wants me to behave?"

How did the challenge go? What did you learn?

WEEK 16

HOW CAN I HAVE A RELATIONSHIP WITH GOD?

This is the covenant that I will make with the house of Israel after those days, declares the Lord: I will put my law within them, and I will write it on their hearts. And I will be their God, and they shall be my people. And no longer shall each one teach his neighbor and each his brother, saying, "Know the Lord," for they shall all know me, from the least of them to the greatest, declares the Lord. For I will forgive their iniquity, and I will remember their sin no more.

—JEREMIAH 31:33–34

LESSON TO LEARN

God wants a relationship with you.

DAY 1

Technology is everywhere. Smartphones have become our most important devices. We use them to make phone calls, send text messages, check emails, take pictures, listen to music, play games, get directions, and watch movies. Some people even use their phones to do their work. When something isn't working quite right on our phones, one of the first things we do to fix the problem is update our apps.

The Israelites had a terrible time trying to keep their covenant with God. The problem was not God's covenant but the people's bad habits. So God decided to update the covenant so we could keep it.

Do you remember what the word *covenant* means? It's a promise. In the old covenant God promised to take care of his people if they were loyal to him. We can see from the Garden of Eden that God's plan was to live among his people. But when they were disloyal, the plan needed to change. Under the old covenant, people could receive forgiveness for their sins through sacrificing an animal. Although people were thankful for this gift of forgiveness, the process never ended. They continued making sacrifices because they continued messing up. God updated his covenant with two important upgrades: First, unlike the animals of old, Jesus was a perfect sacrifice to cover all our sins. Second, God put the Holy Spirit in our hearts to guide and teach us.

With the updated covenant came three advantages for Christians:

1. We get to have a personal relationship with Jesus, so we don't need a priest to be the middleman between us and God.
2. Our sins are forgiven. All of them. All our past sins and all our future sins are forgiven because of Jesus's sacrifice on the cross.
3. Because the Holy Spirit lives in us, he guides us to live more like Jesus lived.

CHALLENGE

Each time you disobey your parents this week, do ten pushups. Let this be a fun reminder that you don't have to do anything to receive forgiveness from God. Jesus *is* the perfect sacrifice.

DAY 2

God updated his covenant so we can have a real relationship with him.

MEMORY WORK

I will put my law within them, and I will write it on their hearts. And I will be their God, and they shall be my people.
—JEREMIAH 31:33

DAY 3

READ MATTHEW 3:13–17.

Why did John the Baptist not want to baptize Jesus?

If Jesus was sinless, why did he want to be baptized?

Why is baptism such a big decision?

DAY 4

READ LUKE 4:1–13.

What happened after Jesus was baptized?

Does being baptized mean we will never face hard things? Is it easier to live for Christ after being baptized?

Why would Satan tempt someone after they've decided to give their life to Christ?

DAY 5

MENTORING MOMENT

MENTOR “What makes relationships successful?”

CHILD “What makes relationships difficult?”

MENTOR “What makes you feel special in a friendship? How does God provide that?”

CHILD “How can I feel close to God when life is hard?”

MENTOR “What role do you play in having a relationship with God?”

CHILD “What makes a relationship with God difficult?”

CHALLENGE CHECK

How did the challenge go? What did you learn?

WEEK 17

WHY DID
JESUS
BECOME
HUMAN
LIKE US?

Behold, with the clouds of heaven
there came one like a son of man.

—DANIEL 7:13

LESSON TO LEARN

Jesus lived humbly as an example for us to follow.

DAY 1

Son of Man? Wait a second! Isn't Jesus supposed to be the Son of *God*? If you've been to church, you've probably heard that Jesus is God's Son and therefore fully God. But he was also Mary's son, and that made him fully human. How is this possible? It's hard to wrap our brains around, but then again, so are many things Jesus did: walking on water, raising people from the dead, and feeding thousands of people with only five loaves of bread and two fish. Our God specializes in doing the impossible!

In Jesus's day, to call someone "son of man" was to point out his human limitations rather than his strengths. It wasn't exactly an insult, but it also wasn't a compliment. Jesus had no problem calling himself "Son of Man," though. You know who else called Jesus "Son of Man"? No one! No one else pointed out his weakness, his humanness. But he knew he had to become like us, knowing our human struggles and human hurt, so that we could become like him.

Why would Jesus, who is fully God, want to leave heaven to come to earth? Simple: because he loves you. You are his favorite part of creation. He loves you so much that he was willing to leave the perfection and comfort of heaven to show you how his love can change your life.

Jesus did that for us, and he wants us to follow his example and do it for others. We definitely aren't God, and our sacrifices aren't going to be anywhere close to Jesus's, but loving others often requires us to give up some sort of comfort. Maybe it's giving up the comfort of the normal friends you sit with at school to sit with someone who is alone. Maybe it's sacrificing your allowance to help a family be able to have a Thanksgiving meal. Maybe it's sacrificing sleeping in so you can help your family pick up the yard. There are a lot of ways to give up your comfort in order to show others the love of God. There is only one God, but we can all be examples of his love to the world.

CHALLENGE

Give up one of your comforts this week for someone else's benefit.

DAY 2

Jesus is God in the flesh. His example teaches us how to love people as God loves them.

MEMORY WORK

Behold, with the clouds of heaven there came one like a son of man.
—DANIEL 7:13

DAY 3

READ DANIEL 3:1-6, 12-30.

What comfort were Shadrach, Meshach, and Abednego willing to give up to bring God glory?

How did Shadrach, Meshach, and Abednego's choices affect other people?

Do you think Shadrach, Meshach, and Abednego knew God would save them? How did God honor their choice to stand firm in their faith?

DAY 4

READ DANIEL 6.

What comfort was Daniel willing to give up to bring God glory?

How did Daniel's choice affect other people?

Do you think Daniel was afraid? How did God honor his choice to stand firm in his faith?

DAY 5

MENTORING MOMENT

MENTOR "How can you give up your comfort today to show God's love to someone?"

CHILD "What's one way you've experienced God doing the impossible in your life?"

MENTOR "Have you ever felt like you were the only person trying to make a choice that honored God?"

CHILD "How do you think God will honor my choices to stand firm in my faith?"

MENTOR "Where do you need to take a stronger stand for your faith?"

CHILD "What do I need to be prepared to lose when I stand firm in my faith?"

CHALLENGE CHECK

How did the challenge go? What did you learn?

WHAT DOES IT TAKE TO BE HAPPY?

People will say bad things about you and hurt you. They will lie and say all kinds of evil things about you because you follow me. But when they do these things to you, you are happy. Rejoice and be glad. You have a great reward waiting for you in heaven. People did the same evil things to the prophets who lived before you.

—MATTHEW 5:11–12, ICB

LESSON TO LEARN

Sometimes what will make you really happy is what you least expect.

DAY 1

What are some things that bring you happiness? Go ahead and list them out loud right now.

You probably included things like family, friends, and your favorite activities. It's easy to see how the things on your list bring happiness. But Jesus's list in Matthew 5 looks much different from ours. Jesus's list goes something like this: happy are those who know they have spiritual needs, happy are those who are sad now, happy are the humble, happy are those who want to do right, happy are the merciful, happy are the pure in heart, happy are the peacemakers, and happy are the persecuted—those who are treated badly because they follow Jesus.

Happy are the persecuted? Has Jesus lost his mind? Far from it. Jesus knows something that we often forget. Being popular and having cool things can't give you lasting happiness. Sure, they can make you happy for a moment. But soon you'll just want the next thing. What did you get for Christmas last year? Chances are that you played with it a lot and treated it with extra care at first. But as time went by, its newness wore off and it became just another thing in your pile of things. You might not even play with it anymore. And you probably have a new wish list going.

Jesus has the recipe for happiness that lasts—a relationship with him! Let's walk through Jesus's list again and see how it builds a relationship that brings permanent happiness.

Happy are those who know they have spiritual needs. Sometimes we like to imagine that we achieve things on our own because we're smart or athletic or hardworking. But the truth is that we can't do any of it without God. The more aware we become of our needs, the more we realize that God is our provider.

Happy are those who are sad now. We should always turn to God for comfort. But sometimes it takes experiencing deep sadness to remember just how much God is there for us.

Happy are the humble. The story of the tortoise and the hare comes to mind. The quiet strength of the tortoise outlasted the in-your-face attitude of the hare. The quiet strength of the humble will eventually win the race of life.

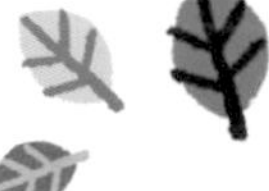

Happy are those who want to do right. Just like Christmas presents, new stuff gets old. Fashion trends change; video games become outdated; even friendships can change. None of those things keep us fulfilled in the long run. But seeking God and his righteousness will.

Happy are the merciful. When you share a toy or game with a friend, it probably will make your friend want to share something with you. The same is true of God. God is merciful, and when we show mercy to others, he wants to share his mercy with us.

Happy are the pure in heart. *Pure* means "clean or sinless." Although we aren't sinless, we can work toward having a pure heart with kind thoughts, language, and actions. This is a reward in itself.

Happy are the peacemakers. With more peace on earth, maybe wars wouldn't be necessary. This is a lovely thought. It may seem impossible for you to do anything about bringing peace to the whole world, but what can you do to bring peace to your family or your group of friends?

Happy are the persecuted. When we suffer for God, he is present with us. It's better to have only God as your friend than be super popular without him.

CHALLENGE

Find a missionary that your church supports. Write them a letter of encouragement.

DAY 2

God wants to give you his true and lasting happiness.

MEMORY WORK

People will say bad things about you and hurt you. They will lie and say all kinds of evil things about you because you follow me. But when they do these things to you, you are happy.
—MATTHEW 5:11, ICB

DAY 3

READ JOHN 3:1–21.

How do you think God would define happiness for us?

This chapter contains one of the most famous Bible verses, John 3:16. What kind of happiness is promised to us in this verse, and how do we get it?

Why do some people who seem to have everything not have happiness?

DAY 4

READ JOHN 4:1–42.

In verse 14, Jesus wasn't talking about actual water. What do you think he was talking about?

In verse 35, Jesus began to talk about a harvest. What was he really talking about?

How is Jesus's list in Matthew 5 different from how most people define happiness?

DAY 5

MENTORING MOMENT

MENTOR "What are some similarities and differences between your list of what brings happiness and Jesus's list of what brings happiness?"

CHILD "Have you ever experienced a blessing from God that the world wouldn't consider a blessing?"

MENTOR "Which item on Jesus's list gives you the most hope? Why?"

CHILD "How can I get better at being happy the way Jesus wants me to?"

MENTOR "Which part of Jesus's list do you need to practice most?"

CHILD "Which part of Jesus's list do you think I model most?"

CHALLENGE CHECK

How did the challenge go?
What did you learn?

HOW CAN I BE A GOOD PERSON?

I tell you, unless your righteousness exceeds that of the scribes and Pharisees, you will never enter the kingdom of heaven.

—MATTHEW 5:20

LESSON TO LEARN

God measures goodness by your heart, not just your actions.

DAY 1

Jesus said we have to be more righteous than the Pharisees. Yikes! The Pharisees were *very* religious. It was basically their job to be good. How could we possibly be more righteous than the professionals? We can't give more money or pray more than they did. Maybe the answer is to do more kind deeds? No. These men were experts in perfect actions. But Jesus is less interested in actions and more interested in the motives of your heart. Let's look at three examples:

First, the law says, "Do not murder." I'd say that most of us have avoided that. Maybe we've even avoided throwing punches. But Jesus's way isn't just about avoiding what's wrong. It's more about doing what's right with the right attitude. Can you have an angry, hateful attitude toward someone without throwing a punch? Absolutely. Jesus wants us to get to the root of the problem. He wants us to learn how to control our tempers before they lead us to harmful attitudes and behaviors. He wants us to love our brothers and sisters, not just avoid punching them.

Second, the law allows people to get even. So, in Moses's day, if your brother broke your toy, you could break his toy. We probably operate with this "they did it first" mentality a lot. But Jesus tells us that if someone strikes us, we should turn the other cheek. It's the opposite of what our human nature wants to do. But it's healthy for our hearts to learn to love under all circumstances.

Third might be the hardest example of all. The law says to love your neighbors and hate your enemies, but Jesus said to love your enemies so that you can be like God. Loving our neighbors seems easy. Loving those who treat us badly gets a lot more difficult! But didn't God love us when we didn't deserve it? Even when we weren't showing love to him? God wants us to imitate his love for all people, even when they don't deserve it.

CHALLENGE

This week, pray for someone who is hard for you to get along with.

DAY 2

God measures goodness by your heart, not just your actions. When your heart is pure, your actions will follow suit.

MEMORY WORK

I tell you, unless your righteousness exceeds that of the scribes and Pharisees, you will never enter the kingdom of heaven.
—MATTHEW 5:20

DAY 3

READ JUDGES 15:1–17.

In this chapter, we see someone getting even. But was it really even, or did things just keep getting more violent?

How might this story have ended differently if Samson had been able to deal with his anger in a healthy way?

What will be required of you to bring peace when you feel like getting even?

DAY 4

READ JUDGES 16:4–22.

What's an example of doing the right thing with the wrong attitude?

What's the difference between doing what's right and avoiding what's wrong?

Think about what you can learn from Samson's life. What's a situation where you need to do what's right rather than just try to avoid what's wrong?

DAY 5

MENTORING MOMENT

MENTOR "What pulls your heart in the wrong direction? Is it selfishness, anger, pride, or greed?"

CHILD "What can I do to help my heart and my behavior match?"

MENTOR "Why does God care about your heart more than your actions?"

CHILD "Do you think Jesus ever wanted to get even?"

MENTOR "Why is getting even so dangerous?"

CHILD "Do you ever have to fight the urge to get even?"

CHALLENGE CHECK

How did the challenge go? What did you learn?

WEEK 20

HOW SHOULD I PRAY?

Our Father in heaven,
hallowed be your name.
Your kingdom come,
your will be done,
on earth as it is in heaven.
Give us this day our daily bread,
and forgive us our debts,
as we also have forgiven
our debtors.
And lead us not into temptation,
but deliver us from evil.

—MATTHEW 6:9–13

LESSON TO LEARN

God wants you to learn how to talk to him.

DAY 1

Have you ever listened to babies learning to talk? They start by babbling. Eventually that babbling resembles real words. The more they practice, the clearer their words become, and they start to string three or four words together to form short sentences. We don't expect newborn babies to know how to talk. It takes time for them to learn. The same is true with our prayer lives. We have to learn how to pray. There are no magic words that we need to pray, but there is a model that can help us learn to pray like Jesus. This model is our memory work for the week. Let's break it down:

1. **Our Father in heaven** We should talk to God in heaven as we would talk to a good father on earth. A good earthly father is a reflection of our perfect heavenly Father. He created us, he provides for us, and he wants what's best for us. Knowing we can be close to our strong, protective heavenly Father brings us comfort.
2. **Hallowed be your name** *Hallowed* is another word for "holy." We can have a personal relationship with God and call him Father, but we also need to honor his holiness. In other words, we should praise him. So, get creative! Think of other words you could use as well as *holy. God, you are worthy. God, you are strong. God, you are enough.* Compliment God for his character. God will love hearing you praise him as much as you love it when people praise you.
3. **Your kingdom come, your will be done, on earth as it is in heaven** We declare our trust in God and say that we are willing to serve him. He won't always answer our prayers the way we want them to be answered. But we still trust him. We trust that he will answer our prayers the way that is best for his kingdom.
4. **Give us this day our daily bread** Ask God to give you what you need to get the job done. What's the job? It will look different for

CHALLENGE

Write out your prayer requests. Cross off all the requests that don't make Jesus famous. Notice what you're left with.

everyone, but at the core, the job of all Christians is to make the name of Jesus famous. To spread the love of God to the whole world. When your prayer aligns with what God wants, he will always say yes. Here's a cool idea (this is our challenge this week): Write out your prayer requests. Cross off all the requests that don't make Jesus famous. You'll be left with the prayers that God wants to answer with a *yes*. This doesn't mean that God can't or won't answer your prayer to win the soccer game, pass the test, or feel better when you're sick. But God wants you to look beyond what *you* want. It's good to practice thinking about some prayer requests that will align with God's mission for the whole world.

5. **Forgive us our debts, as we also have forgiven our debtors** It's easy to focus on the first part of this sentence and skip over the last part. God wants to forgive us, but he also wants us to forgive people who have hurt us. This can be very hard to do. It may be a long journey of forgiveness. But you have to begin. If you aren't ready to forgive, ask God to help you want to forgive. If that still seems like too big of a step, start by thanking God for forgiving you when you have sinned.
6. **Lead us not into temptation, but deliver us from evil** Sometimes it's really hard to do what's right. Not picking on your brother or sister, doing your chores, obeying your parents. It may seem impossible. But if you ask God for help, he will always give you the strength and wisdom you need to live a life that honors him.

DAY 2

God wants us to learn how to talk to him so much that he gave us instructions. The more we practice, the easier it will become.

MEMORY WORK

Our Father in heaven,
hallowed be your name.
Your kingdom come,
your will be done,
on earth as it is in heaven.
Give us this day our daily bread,
and forgive us our debts,
as we also have forgiven our debtors.
And lead us not into temptation,
but deliver us from evil.
—MATTHEW 6:9–13

DAY 3

READ JOHN 17.

It's clear that Jesus's prayer is aligned with what God wants. Does Jesus pray more for himself or for others?

It's hard to get better at something if you don't practice. How often do you practice praying?

How do you know if your prayers are aligned with what God wants?

DAY 4

Practice praying by using the guide Jesus has given us, but use your own words.

- Address God as Father.
- Praise God.
- Declare your trust in God's plan.
- Ask for what you need.
- Ask for forgiveness (and then offer forgiveness).
- Ask for the strength to do what's right.

CHALLENGE CHECK

How did the challenge go?
What did you learn?

DAY 5

MENTORING MOMENT

MENTOR "Out of the six parts of the model prayer, which do your prayers look most like?"

CHILD "When do you pray? Where do you pray? What do you pray about? How do you pray?"

MENTOR "Which of the six parts of the model prayer do you spend the least amount of time on?"

CHILD "Do prayers always have to have all six parts?"

MENTOR "How is your prayer life?"

CHILD "Why is prayer important?"

WEEK 21

WHY DOES MY MONEY MATTER TO GOD?

Lay up for yourselves treasures in heaven, where neither moth nor rust destroys and where thieves do not break in and steal. For where your treasure is, there your heart will be also.

—MATTHEW 6:20–21

LESSON TO LEARN

Everything we have belongs to God.

DAY 1

Money is important to God. After all, he talked about it in 2,300 Bible verses. Compare that with prayer, which he talked about in five hundred verses. Now, God doesn't care about how much money you have. He cares about how much it has you.

That's why God tells us to tithe. A tithe is when you give back to God the first 10 percent of what you get. If you made ten dollars by selling lemonade to people in your neighborhood, you would tithe one dollar back to your church. Tithing isn't always easy, but it's always healthy.

Some people say, "But it's my money!" Actually, it's not. Psalm 24:1 says, "The earth is the Lord's, and everything in it. The world and all its people belong to him" (NLT). That means the whole ten dollars is actually God's. You're not *giving* him a tithe; you're *returning* the first 10 percent of what he blessed you with.

You see, we don't really own our money; we just manage it for God. That's called stewardship. Jesus said if we are faithful with little, God will give us more. It's like when you show you can keep your room clean, your parents might let you get a dog. Or if you do your chores, you get to have a friend over. It's the same with God and money. When God sees that we can be good stewards of small amounts of money, he will want to give us more money to manage.

Some people might not tithe because they think, *God doesn't need my money.* That's true. God doesn't need your money. But he wants your heart. Matthew 6:24 tells us that we can't serve both God and money. We have to make a choice. That's why one of our memory verses for this week says, "Where your treasure is, there your heart will be also" (verse 21). God is telling us that if we serve money, we can't also serve him as Lord of our lives. God's commands about money aren't actually about money at all. They're about what controls our hearts.

CHALLENGE

Choose a special place to keep the first 10 percent of any money you get. Don't forget to take it to church to give it back to God.

DAY 2

God cares less about your money and more about what has control of your heart.

MEMORY WORK

Lay up for yourselves treasures in heaven, where neither moth nor rust destroys and where thieves do not break in and steal. For where your treasure is, there your heart will be also.
—MATTHEW 6:20–21

DAY 3

READ GENESIS 14:13–24.

Who did Abram give credit to for his blessings? Who do you give credit to for your blessings?

If God doesn't need our money, why does he ask for it?

Money isn't the only thing that can rule our hearts. Is there another area of your life that you need to give to God?

DAY 4

READ MALACHI 3:6–12.

How does God want us to test him?

Why is giving a tithe hard to do? Why is it important?

If you feel like God has changed (see verse 6), what's probably the real problem?

DAY 5

MENTORING MOMENT

MENTOR "What are your three favorite things? Can you think of how they actually came from God?"

CHILD "Can you help me set up a budget so I can tithe?"

MENTOR "What abilities, experiences, and resources are you thankful for? How can you show your thankfulness?"

CHILD "How does tithing help money not rule your heart?"

MENTOR "How can you store up treasures in heaven?"

CHILD "Is tithing easy for you? Why or why not?"

CHALLENGE CHECK

How did the challenge go? What did you learn?

WHAT DOES A CHRISTIAN LIFE LOOK LIKE?

Whatever you wish that others would do to you, do also to them, for this is the Law and the Prophets.

—MATTHEW 7:12

LESSON TO LEARN

God cares more about the good you do for others than the bad things you don't do.

DAY 1

Imagine that you're playing with your friends at the pool. Things get a little rowdy, and all of a sudden, a game of tag starts. Your mom yells, "Don't run!" You know exactly what she means—she wants you to walk. However, you could skip, hop, crawl, roll, or tango, and you'd still technically be following her directions.

You probably know the Golden Rule: treat others how you want to be treated. This rule was first spoken by Jesus. But before Jesus taught about the Golden Rule, most people lived by the Silver Rule. The Silver Rule says, "*Don't* do to others what you *don't* want done to you." It sounds so similar to the Golden Rule, but following these two rules looks very different.

If you're living by the Silver Rule, you simply need to avoid mistreating others. You could stay home all day and play video games and still be following the Silver Rule. But this would be serving only yourself. However, if you're following the Golden Rule, you need to seek out ways to serve others. James 1:27 says, "Religion that God our Father accepts as pure and faultless is this: to look after orphans and widows in their distress and to keep oneself from being polluted by the world" (NIV). God doesn't just want us to keep from harming people who are in need (the Silver Rule). He wants us to take care of them (the Golden Rule). What would it look like for you to do this in your own community?

CHALLENGE

Do something kind for one person you don't know personally.

DAY 2

God cares more about the good you do for others (the Golden Rule) than the bad things you don't do (the Silver Rule).

MEMORY WORK

Whatever you wish that others would do to you, do also to them, for this is the Law and the Prophets.
—MATTHEW 7:12

DAY 3

READ MICAH 6:8.

What's the difference between the Golden Rule and the Silver Rule?

What makes it hard to love someone?

Think of all the people you encountered this past week that Jesus would consider your neighbors. How well did you do with treating them like neighbors?

DAY 4

READ JAMES 1:27.

Who does God call us to take care of?

What does the way we treat others say about our faith?

Why would God detest religion that isn't pure and faultless?

DAY 5

MENTORING MOMENT

MENTOR "Do you live more by the Golden Rule or the Silver Rule with your friends? With your family? With strangers? With people you don't get along with?"

CHILD "Is the Silver Rule bad?"

MENTOR "What's one way you can live out the Golden Rule today?"

CHILD "How can I change my Silver Rule actions into Golden Rule actions?"

MENTOR "Do you have an easier time living by the Golden Rule with your family or with your friends?"

CHILD "Is God disappointed in me if I live by the Silver Rule rather than the Golden Rule?"

CHALLENGE CHECK

How did the challenge go?
What did you learn?

HOW CAN I SACRIFICE LIKE JESUS?

Jesus told his disciples, "If anyone would come after me, let him deny himself and take up his cross and follow me. For whoever would save his life will lose it, but whoever loses his life for my sake will find it."

—MATTHEW 16:24–25

LESSON TO LEARN

Jesus died for us so we could live for others.

DAY 1

Q: What has a head and a tail but no body?
A: A coin.
Q: What belongs to you but your friends use it more?
A: Your name.
Q: How can you save your life by losing it?
A: Keep reading to find the answer.

Sometimes the Bible feels like a riddle that we need to solve. Matthew 16 is one of those examples. This probably felt even more like a riddle to the disciples. Jesus had just finished saying that he would die and rise again three days later. They probably knew what a cross was, but they would never have imagined that Jesus would be crucified on one. Would they have understood the word picture of taking up their crosses to follow Jesus? Was Jesus saying that they needed to die on a cross in order to be saved? If so, what does that mean for us?

Thankfully Jesus wasn't talking about a literal cross for his disciples or us. But the death he was talking about can still be painful. We need to do more than just remember Jesus's sacrifice as something he did for us. We need to imitate it. We can't die for the sins of the world, but we can be less selfish for the good of others.

What does your cross look like? We will all have to make different sacrifices. It might be putting to death your cool-kid reputation at school to be a friend to a kid who doesn't have as many friends as you. It might look like not getting the new shoes that just came out so you can help a student pay for church camp next summer. It might look like swallowing your pride and telling your sister that you're sorry. Some sacrifices might feel like a paper cut, while others might feel like an amputation. But if we want to be followers of Jesus, we have to be willing to imitate his actions.

So, how can you save your life by losing it? Stop living by *your* ways. Turn to Jesus and living according to his ways.

CHALLENGE

Let someone else have their way. Let a sibling choose what's for dinner; let your friend pick the game you play; let your dad pick the music in the car.

DAY 2

Jesus was the ultimate sacrifice so we could be forgiven of our sins. As his followers, we are called to imitate his actions.

MEMORY WORK

Jesus told his disciples, "If anyone would come after me, let him deny himself and take up his cross and follow me. For whoever would save his life will lose it, but whoever loses his life for my sake will find it."
—MATTHEW 16:24–25

DAY 3

READ MARK 15:1–32.

In this story, was following the crowd the easy thing to do? Was it the right thing to do?

How is giving up something we want imitating Jesus?

Why is doing the right thing often so hard?

DAY 4

READ MARK 15:33–39.

Why did Jesus feel like God had abandoned him? Had God abandoned him?

When have you felt the most alone? Had God abandoned you?

Jesus gave his life on the cross. How did that sacrifice save us?

DAY 5

MENTORING MOMENT

MENTOR "What's the greatest sacrifice someone has ever made for you?"

CHILD "What's the most painful sacrifice you've ever made?"

MENTOR "What's the biggest sacrifice you've ever made?"

CHILD "What have you learned from making sacrifices?"

MENTOR "What's one sacrifice you need to make?"

CHILD "Does making sacrifices mean that I never get my way?"

CHALLENGE CHECK

How did the challenge go? What did you learn?

WEEK 24

DOES GOD WANT ME?

Many are called, but few are chosen.

—MATTHEW 22:14

LESSON TO LEARN

God chose you.

DAY 1

Can you imagine being the president of the United States of America? One person is president for four years before our country chooses the next president. We call this process an election. To be elected means to be chosen. Kings and queens also lead countries, but they aren't elected. No one votes for the king or queen. The reigning king and queen have a baby, and that baby becomes the heir to the throne simply by being born.

The Bible talks about God choosing us. Christians often use two big words to talk about this: *election* and *predestination*. They mean the same thing: God chooses you. The question is, Do you have a choice? Jesus actually answered this question in Matthew 22:14. He said, "Many are called, but few are chosen." There you have it. The Bible says few are chosen, right? God must have elected the people he wants to go to heaven. Not so fast.

Jesus was telling a story about a man who decided to throw a party. The man invited a lot of people. In fact, he sent his servants out into the town and instructed them to invite everyone they saw. If someone didn't go to the party, it was because that person didn't want to go. We can look at our invitation to heaven in the same way. God invites us all to heaven. And we get to decide whether we will accept the invitation.

God already knows who will accept the invitation. He knows how you will respond. Has your mom ever told you that she has eyes in the back of her head? She doesn't really—she just knows you really, really well. Sometimes she can anticipate your actions before you even do them. Just because your mom knows what you're about to do doesn't mean that she controls your choice. It just means that she knows you really, really well, even better than you know yourself sometimes. Wouldn't you think that God, our Creator, knows us really, really well

CHALLENGE

It seems like overnight Saul went from threatening Christians to preaching about Jesus (Acts 9). Pretend that you're Saul, and write a diary entry about the recent life-changing events.

too? He doesn't make our choices for us, but he does know what we will do before we actually do it.

God has invited all of us to join him in heaven. The invitation comes with responsibilities, like honoring him and loving our neighbors. Some people won't want to accept the responsibilities. But everyone gets the invitation.

DAY 2

God invites everyone. Accepting the invitation is a personal choice.

MEMORY WORK

Many are called, but few are chosen.
—MATTHEW 22:14

DAY 3

READ ACTS 9:1–16.

 Why were Christians afraid of Saul?

 What was Saul predestined (or chosen) for?

 What does Saul's story reveal to us about who God invites to be saved?

DAY 4

READ ACTS 9:17–31.

 What do you think the disciples were thinking when Saul first claimed to be a Christian?

 What challenges did Saul face because he accepted Jesus's invitation?

 What challenges might you face because you've accepted Jesus's invitation?

DAY 5

MENTORING MOMENT

MENTOR "What makes you feel chosen?"

CHILD "Have you ever been afraid to live for Jesus?"

MENTOR "What does God want to use you for?"

CHILD "Will God choose some people for the same things?"

MENTOR "Is it your job to get people to come to Jesus or to invite them to know Jesus?"

CHILD "Why do some people refuse the invitation to know Jesus?"

CHALLENGE CHECK ___

How did the challenge go?
What did you learn?

WEEK 25

IS THE
SUPERNATURAL
WORLD
ACTUALLY
REAL?

He will say to those on his left, "Depart from me, you cursed, into the eternal fire prepared for the devil and his angels."

—MATTHEW 25:41

LESSON TO LEARN

Angels and demons are real even if we can't see them.

DAY 1

Have you ever thought about why we have locks on our homes? Some people even have security systems or cameras installed around their properties to try to keep themselves and their belongings safe. Most of the time burglars will move on to the next house that feels a little less protected. Maybe they'll even find a house that was left unlocked. Sometimes burglars have their eyes on something in a specific home, like a big-screen TV. If they want it badly enough, they'll wear a disguise and have a very specific plan so they don't get caught.

That's kind of like what demons do all around us. Satan and his demons are in the business of stealing people away from God.

They might go door to door (person to person) until they come across an unlocked door (heart). Or they might target a specific individual and come up with a well-thought-out plan.

The good news is that God has given us security systems for our hearts. We don't have to leave our doors unlocked and cross our fingers that we will be safe. We have ways to protect ourselves from the evil that wants to steal our hearts away from God.

The first security measure we have is the Bible. The Bible is full of truth and God's promises to us. Reading and memorizing Scripture can help protect our hearts from danger. The second security measure is praising God through song. Oftentimes hymns and worship music are Bible verses set to melodies so that they are easier and more fun to repeat. Even if the songs aren't actual Scripture, they can hold the same reminder of God's truth and promises. The third security measure is prayer. Praying in Jesus's name is a very powerful tool against evil. And whether you see them or not, there are angels ready to protect you (Hebrews 1:14). An unseen yet very real battle is going on for your heart. Don't forget to lock up!

CHALLENGE

Listen to only worship music this week.

DAY 2

An unseen battle is being fought for your heart. But God has given you ways to win.

MEMORY WORK

He will say to those on his left, "Depart from me, you cursed, into the eternal fire prepared for the devil and his angels."
—MATTHEW 25:41

DAY 3

READ HEBREWS 1.

 What do you think angels are like?

 What do angels do for us?

 Do you think humans are more important to God than angels? Explain.

DAY 4

READ REVELATION 13.

 In your favorite movie, who/what do the villains care about? Who or what do the heroes care about?

 How would an angel want you to treat other people? What would a demon want you to do to other people?

 How does this passage reveal that a spiritual battle is going on for your heart?

DAY 5

MENTORING MOMENT

MENTOR "What are ways to lock our hearts against the enemy?"

CHILD "What habits do you have that protect your faith?"

MENTOR "Just as there are ways to lock our hearts against the enemy, there are also behaviors that leave our hearts unlocked for the enemy to walk right in. What are some behaviors that might leave your heart unlocked?"

CHILD "Have you ever been afraid of the supernatural world? What did you do?"

MENTOR "What behavior that leaves your heart unlocked is hardest for you to give up?"

CHILD "What habits should I start practicing to protect my faith?"

CHALLENGE CHECK

How did the challenge go? What did you learn?

WEEK 26

WHAT'S GOD'S PURPOSE FOR ME?

All authority in heaven and on earth has been given to me. Go therefore and make disciples of all nations, baptizing them in the name of the Father and of the Son and of the Holy Spirit, teaching them to observe all that I have commanded you. And behold, I am with you always, to the end of the age.

—MATTHEW 28:18–20

LESSON TO LEARN

We are partners with God in sharing Jesus.

DAY 1

What do the words *copilot*, *coworker*, and *cooperate* have in common? They all start with the prefix *co*, and they all have something to do with teamwork or togetherness. A copilot helps the pilot fly the plane, a coworker is someone you help at work, and to cooperate means you work with someone else to accomplish a job. Our memory verse this week is what we call the Great Commission. (There's that *co* again!) God has tasked Christians with the mission of making disciples. But before it was our mission, it was *his* mission. He invites us to be copilots on his mission.

This mission sounds exciting, but how do we get started? The Great Commission tells people to go, but God doesn't mean you need to move to Africa or sign up for every mission trip. Those are good things to do, but God isn't necessarily asking that of you. He's asking you to make Jesus famous while you do the things you're already doing. When you're at school, make Jesus famous. When you're at practice, make Jesus famous. When you're playing at the park, make Jesus famous. How? By following the two greatest commandments: love God and love others. Your goal doesn't have to be baptizing every person you meet. It just needs to be helping at least one person take one step closer to God. If this mission makes you nervous, just remember that it's not *your* mission. It's God's mission. And God even finishes off the Great Commission with an amazing promise: "I am with you always, to the end of the age."

CHALLENGE

Name one person you would like to help take one step closer to Jesus. Pray for that person every day this week.

DAY 2

We are partners with God in sharing Jesus and making him famous.

MEMORY WORK

Go therefore and make disciples of all nations.
—MATTHEW 28:19

What does it look like for you to make Jesus famous?

Why does God want us to be his partners?

DAY 3

Compare Acts 1:8 to the Great Commission. What do they have in common?

You will receive power when the Holy Spirit has come upon you, and you will be my witnesses in Jerusalem and in all Judea and Samaria, and to the end of the earth. —ACTS 1:8

DAY 4

Choose a verse from yesterday to put into your own words.

If you were to brag about Jesus to one of your friends, what would you say?

Jesus sent people out in pairs. Can you think of one friend from church who is also friends with the person you want to invite to church?

DAY 5

MENTORING MOMENT

MENTOR "How can you make Jesus famous today?"

CHILD "Have you ever led someone to Christ? What led up to that?"

MENTOR "How does it make you feel knowing that God wants to partner with you?"

CHILD "How has God been able to use you as his partner in the Great Commission?"

MENTOR "Is there anyone you would like to invite to church with us?"

CHILD "Is there anyone you would like to invite to church with us?"

CHALLENGE CHECK

How did the challenge go?
What did you learn?

WEEK 27

WHY IS CHRISTIANITY GOOD NEWS?

This is the Good News about Jesus the Messiah, the Son of God.

—MARK 1:1, NLT

LESSON TO LEARN

Jesus is our king on earth, not just a savior in heaven.

DAY 1

Have you ever listened to someone tell a story and thought to yourself, *That's not how that happened!* We've probably all been there because we all experience things from our own perspectives. We could attend the same concert but have different seats that give us different views. We could witness the same event but remember different details. We even see this play out in the Bible.

Matthew, Mark, Luke, and John are the first four books of the New Testament. Some stories appear in only one of these books. But many stories can be found in three or four of them, just written from a different person's perspective. Matthew and John were two of Jesus's twelve disciples. Some of their stories are firsthand accounts of things they got to witness with their own eyes. Mark met Jesus near the end of his ministry, but Luke never did; he wrote his accounts after investigating other people's experiences.

These four books, also called the Gospels, tell the story of Jesus. But they're more than just stories. The term *gospel* means "good news." Originally it was used for political events like winning a war or the emperor getting married or having a baby. So, why is the story of Jesus described as good political news? Because it isn't just about our savior; it's about our king. Jesus is the king of our hearts, not just a savior in heaven.

Jesus will use you to expand his kingdom on earth. That will look different for each of us, just as the four gospel writers had their own perspectives and experiences. But all of us are his ambassadors. It's our job to spread the good news wherever we go: our king has won the greatest victory ever, over sin and death.

CHALLENGE

Separately ask your parents (or another couple you know) how they met. Take note of the differences and similarities in their stories.

DAY 2

Jesus is our king on earth, not just a savior in heaven. We don't have to wait for his return to let him be the king of our hearts.

MEMORY WORK

This is the Good News about Jesus the Messiah, the Son of God.
—MARK 1:1, NLT

DAY 3

Read at least one of the accounts of Jesus's betrayal and arrest:

MATTHEW 26:47–56; MARK 14:43–52; LUKE 22:47–53; JOHN 18:1–11.

How can Jesus's kingdom expand on earth if his kingdom is in heaven?

Why does Jesus care more about being king of your heart than being king of a country?

If Jesus is king, what are your obligations to him?

DAY 4

Read a different account of Jesus's betrayal and arrest than you did yesterday:

MATTHEW 26:47–56; MARK 14:43–52; LUKE 22:47–53; JOHN 18:1–11.

Read at least two of the passages listed. Do they tell the same story? How are they similar? How are they different?

Why does the same story have subtle differences?

Do subtle differences discredit a story?

DAY 5

MENTORING MOMENT

MENTOR "Pretend that you're one of the characters in the story you read on days 3 and 4. Retell the story from his perspective."

CHILD "How has the story of Jesus been good news for our family?"

MENTOR "What part of heaven are you most excited about?"

CHILD "How can you see evidence of God's kingdom here on earth?"

MENTOR "How will God's kingdom in heaven be different from God's kingdom on earth?"

CHILD "Does the thought of heaven ever scare you?"

CHALLENGE CHECK

How did the challenge go? What did you learn?

WEEK 28

WHAT DOES IT MEAN TO BELIEVE?

The time is fulfilled, and the kingdom of God is at hand; repent and believe in the gospel.

—MARK 1:15

LESSON TO LEARN

Faith is putting your belief into action.

DAY 1

Have you ever had a parent, a teacher, or a coach say, "I believe in you"? Did they mean "I believe you exist"? Or did they mean "I have confidence in you, so I'm putting my trust in you"? Of course they meant they trusted you. The same thing is true about faith in Jesus. It's more than believing he exists. It's putting our trust in him. James 2:19 says, "You believe that there is one God. Good! Even the demons believe that—and shudder" (NIV). Demons believe but don't have faith. The difference lies in the definition of the word *faith*. In the Bible, the word for "faith" actually means "loyalty." Demons believe in God, but they don't have loyalty to God.

Loyalty is pledging your allegiance to something. You've probably put your right hand over your heart and said, "I pledge allegiance to the flag . . ." An ordinary citizen may say that pledge routinely, but a soldier has to put the pledge into action. Serving in the military doesn't make someone any more of a citizen than someone who doesn't serve. It is, however, one way to put action to their loyalty. Putting our faith in Jesus is similar.

God calls us to put our loyalty into action. James 2:18 says, "Someone will say, 'You have faith; I have deeds.' Show me your faith without deeds, and I will show you my faith by my deeds" (NIV). While we can't earn forgiveness with good deeds, we can put our loyalty to God into action. When we fully grasp the meaning of pledging our loyalty to God, our good deeds will be a natural outcome of our allegiance to God.

CHALLENGE

Write a pledge to God. You can model it after the Pledge of Allegiance if that helps.

DAY 2

Faith is putting your belief into action.

MEMORY WORK

The time is fulfilled, and the kingdom of God is at hand; repent and believe in the gospel.

—MARK 1:15

DAY 3

READ GENESIS 6:9–22.

 How do you think people treated Noah while he was building the ark?

 When have you been treated poorly for trying to follow God's instructions?

 How can you prepare for a time when it might be hard to be loyal to God because of what people around you are saying or doing?

DAY 4

READ GENESIS 8.

 How did Noah show his loyalty to God when he got off the ark?

 What's one way you can show your loyalty to God?

 How is loyalty an outcome of faith?

DAY 5

MENTORING MOMENT

MENTOR "What will putting your faith into action look like today?"

CHILD "Tell me about a time when you did a good deed for someone because of your loyalty to God."

MENTOR "When is it easiest for you to be loyal to God? Does it depend on who you are around?"

CHILD "Have you ever been afraid to show your loyalty to God? Does it depend on who you are around?"

MENTOR "What holds people back from being loyal to God?"

CHILD "Does God get mad, sad, or disappointed when we aren't loyal to him?"

CHALLENGE CHECK

How did the challenge go?
What did you learn?

WEEK 29

HOW CAN I FIND REST?

The Sabbath was made for man, not man for the Sabbath.
So the Son of Man is lord even of the Sabbath.

—MARK 2:27–28

LESSON TO LEARN

Rest is necessary for worship and relationships.

DAY 1

Have you ever been on a trip so special that you wanted to buy a souvenir to remember it? Or maybe you've kept an old handwritten card from a loved one that has passed away. These keepsakes aren't necessarily special to anyone else, but they are very special to you. They are things you can hold in your hand so you can keep the memories in your heart.

Did you know that God has given you a keepsake from the Garden of Eden? That's right! It's called rest. Rest is so important that God even demonstrated it for us. Genesis 2:2–3 says, "By the seventh day God had finished the work he had been doing; so on the seventh day he rested from all his work. Then God blessed the seventh day and made it holy, because on it he rested from all the work of creating that he had done" (NIV).

Rest is a gift from God. But people don't always treat it like a gift. In Bible times, the Jewish people took their rest seriously. They rested one day a week, the day they called the Sabbath. Religious leaders wanted to help people honor the Sabbath, so they made lots of rules about what was and wasn't allowed that day. The list of rules kept getting longer until the Sabbath felt more like a chore and less like a gift. Jesus broke some of their rules to allow people to really rest. The religious leaders got angry about that. Our memory work this week is from one of the times the Pharisees fought with Jesus about the rules. But Jesus fought for us, reminding us that God created rest for us, not the other way around.

We may not hear much about a Sabbath today, but we do have

CHALLENGE

Choose a day this week to rest together as a family. To prepare, talk about things like "What is a good day to rest as a family?" "What activities make us feel like we really spent time with one another and with God?" "What extra steps do we need to take to prepare for a day of rest?" Then make a plan and carry it out.

weekends and days off. The important thing is not *when* you rest but *that* you rest. You've maybe heard someone say, "I need a weekend after my weekend" or "I need a vacation from my vacation." We work hard and play harder. God's intention was not just that we have time to play but that we have time to worship, to connect with our families, to laugh hard and tell stories. It's not so much about what we do or don't do; it's about making time to spend with God and people we love. Maybe this weekend, you could take an inventory of your activities. Which activities help you connect with God and with family, and which activities are just making you busy and tired?

DAY 2

Rest is a gift God has given us. It's so important that he modeled it. True rest will help you feel closer to God.

MEMORY WORK

The Sabbath was made for man, not man for the Sabbath. So the Son of Man is lord even of the Sabbath.
—Mark 2:27–28

DAY 3

READ MARK 2:23–28.

What are three things that can help you connect with God and with your family? Examples: going on family bike rides, reading a book together, sleeping in. Get creative. There are no wrong answers here.

It's important to know what connects you to God and family. It's also important to know what distracts you or disconnects you from God and family. Brainstorm a list of things that hurt your ability to rest. Examples: last-minute homework, too much screen time, too many extracurricular events.

What's the difference between Sabbath rest and lazy habits?

DAY 4

READ MARK 3:1–6.

How did Jesus bless this man on the Sabbath?

What are three ways you can help bless someone else's Sabbath? Examples: have a family meal together (and you do the dishes for Mom or Dad!), go to church together, let a sibling choose the movie, play a game with your little brother.

How does rest help you feel closer to God?

CHALLENGE CHECK

How did the challenge go? What did you learn?

DAY 5

MENTORING MOMENT

MENTOR "How do we know Sabbath rest is important to God?"

CHILD "How strict is God about Sabbath rules?"

MENTOR "How can we make Sabbath rest a priority in our busy schedule?"

CHILD "What makes you excited about resting as a family?"

MENTOR "What's the point of Sabbath rest?"

CHILD "What can happen if we don't rest?"

WEEK 30

HOW CAN I BE GREAT?

Even the Son of Man came not to be served but to serve, and to give his life as a ransom for many.

—MARK 10:45

LESSON TO LEARN

The greatest leaders serve those they lead.

DAY 1

Mrs. Hutchinson had been teaching second grade for many years. She was in her fifties and much closer to retirement than any other teacher in the building. Every morning Mrs. Hutchinson would take attendance and then put on her running shoes. She took her class out to the playground, and all together they would run one lap. It didn't matter whether she wore a dress, jeans, or dress pants; Mrs. Hutchinson always ran a lap with her students. It would have been easier to tell her students to run the lap while she stood and waited. There were probably many days that she wanted to stand and wait instead of running. After all, the kids were always happy to get out and run—they probably wouldn't have minded if she'd stood and waited for them to finish. But she never did. She always ran the lap.

What do Mrs. Hutchinson and Jesus have in common? Jesus could have given us a set of rules to follow and left it at that. But he came to earth as a human to experience the same hardships, temptations, and pain and to show us how to live. Jesus had disciples. Just like Mrs. Hutchinson's students would have still run the lap if she had asked them to, Jesus's disciples would have done whatever he asked them to do. But he led by example. Jesus and Mrs. Hutchinson both had positions of power. People in power don't usually run a lap or wash people's feet, right? Imagine for a second how gross that job would be. This was before fingernail clippers or cars were invented. People wore sandals and walked everywhere on dirty, dusty roads. Ew! If Jesus hadn't wanted to wash feet, no one would have thought twice about it. But he led by serving. He was the most powerful man in the room doing the most unwanted job in the room. That is the example of leadership that Jesus has set for us. Leadership doesn't mean that people serve you but rather that you serve others.

CHALLENGE

Do an act of service this week without being asked.

DAY 2

The greatest leaders serve those they lead.

MEMORY WORK

Even the Son of Man came not to be served but to serve, and to give his life as a ransom for many.
—MARK 10:45

DAY 3

READ JOHN 12:1–8.

 What's your most valuable possession? How hard would it be to give up?

 How could you use what you have (time, treasures, talent) to serve others?

 Why did Judas question Mary's action?

DAY 4

READ JOHN 13:1–14.

 What does this story show you about Jesus's leadership?

 How can you serve someone this week by doing a job that no one wants to do?

 Where is it most difficult for you to serve (school, home, church)?

DAY 5

MENTORING MOMENT

MENTOR "Who has been an easy friend or teacher to follow?"

CHILD "Do you see me as a leader?"

MENTOR "How does serving make someone great?"

CHILD "What's an example of successful servant leadership? Why does it work so well?"

MENTOR "What could you do around the house or at school to lead by serving?"

CHILD "What's hard about servant leadership?"

CHALLENGE CHECK

How did the challenge go?
What did you learn?

WEEK 31

WHAT DOES GOD CARE ABOUT MOST?

Jesus answered, "The most important is, 'Hear, O Israel: The Lord our God, the Lord is one. And you shall love the Lord your God with all your heart and with all your soul and with all your mind and with all your strength.' The second is this: 'You shall love your neighbor as yourself.' There is no other commandment greater than these."

—MARK 12:29–31

LESSON TO LEARN

We demonstrate our love for God by loving others.

DAY 1

Isn't it easier to study for a test when you know the questions that are going to be asked? In Mark 12, Jesus gave us the answer to the question "What is the greatest commandment?" The greatest commandment is to love God with all your heart, soul, mind, and strength. And the second greatest commandment is to love your neighbor as yourself. In short, love God and love others. But *knowing* the answer isn't enough to ace this test. Why? Because love isn't an emotion. Love is an action. Think about it. How do you know that your parents love you? Do you know because they tell you, or do you know because they show you? When they take time to listen to you, give you hugs and kisses, and take care of your needs, they are putting their love into action. You can trust their words because their actions prove them.

We also need to put our love for God and others into action. It's impossible to truly love God without loving others. It's also impossible to love God partially. Jesus said he wants us to love God with all our heart, soul, mind, and strength. Jesus included these categories of love to explain that we are to love God with total devotion.

God doesn't play guessing games with us when it comes to what is most important to him. He has given us a very clear answer: love him and love others.

CHALLENGE

Show love this week to a friend or family member in the way that would mean the most to that person. It could be saying kind words, cleaning your room without being asked, having a nice conversation, or even getting them a gift. Be creative.

DAY 2

When we love God and love others, everything else God cares about will fall into line.

MEMORY WORK

"You shall love the Lord your God with all your heart and with all your soul and with all your mind and with all your strength." The second is this: "You shall love your neighbor as yourself."

—MARK 12:30–31

DAY 3

READ EXODUS 20:1–17.

What are the two greatest commandments given by Jesus?

Which of the Ten Commandments are about loving God, and which are about loving people?

If everything falls under the two commandments Jesus mentioned, why did God give ten?

DAY 4

READ LUKE 10:29–37.

Who are your neighbors?

What are some ways you can love your neighbors at home, at school, and in your community?

Why is it impossible to love God without loving people?

DAY 5

MENTORING MOMENT

MENTOR "How did Jesus love his neighbors?"

CHILD "What does it look like to love with my mind, soul, and strength?"

MENTOR "Will you always get love back when you show it?"

CHILD "When have you shown love without being loved back?"

MENTOR "Who do you know that needs an extra dose of God's love? How can you show that person God's love?"

CHILD "What should I do when I feel like I need an extra dose of God's love?"

CHALLENGE CHECK

How did the challenge go? What did you learn?

WEEK 32

IS JESUS GOD?

The Word became flesh and dwelt among us, and we have seen his glory, glory as of the only Son from the Father, full of grace and truth.

—JOHN 1:14

LESSON TO LEARN

God shared our experience so we could experience him.

DAY 1

When you were a baby, you didn't know how to do anything besides cry, eat, and fill your diaper. You had to learn how to talk, walk, eat solid food, and use the toilet. Over those years, your parents spent hours helping you learn these things. They read to you, cut up your food, held your hand, and even ran you to the bathroom countless times a day. Did you know that God did that for us? He met us where we were to teach us his ways and his heart. We call it the Incarnation.

Jesus became a human being. He walked where we walked. He ate the same food, slept, burped, and felt pain. Why? Because he wanted to share our experience so we could someday share his experience. Not that we would become God—we can't—but we can live in his presence because Jesus came to our world to introduce us to the God we couldn't see.

The first lesson we learn through the Incarnation is that God is near. We can pray and have a conversation with him. We don't need anyone to speak to God for us. The next lesson is that *God is love.* God's love reaches both his followers and his enemies. The third lesson is that *God suffered.* Jesus met us where we were and experienced the same earthly pain and discomfort that we experience.

So, how can we transform our lives with these lessons from Jesus's incarnation? We can *be near.* Be present wherever you are. Pause your game or put down your phone, and tune in to conversation with your family or friends. *Love sacrificially.* We learned last week that love is an action. Think of ways that you can show love not only to your friends but also to your enemies. *Embrace suffering.* Discomfort isn't fun. But discomfort and suffering can help us become better versions of ourselves. Instead of complaining about your pain, ask yourself—and God—"What can I learn from this?"

CHALLENGE

As a family, turn off all technology for one hour and just be together.

DAY 2

Through Jesus, God shared our experience so we could experience him.

MEMORY WORK

The Word became flesh and dwelt among us, and we have seen his glory, glory as of the only Son from the Father, full of grace and truth.
—JOHN 1:14

DAY 3

READ MATTHEW 2.

In this scripture, what are the signs that Jesus is God in human form?

How can we know God better because Jesus came to earth?

What's the difference between knowing about someone and knowing someone?

DAY 4

READ LUKE 2:1–21.

In this scripture, what are the signs that Jesus is God in human form?

How can suffering bring you closer to Jesus?

How would the world be different now if Jesus hadn't come to earth?

DAY 5

MENTORING MOMENT

MENTOR "What's one way you've experienced God?"

CHILD "When I was a baby, was it difficult for you to get on my level to help me learn? Why was it worth it?"

MENTOR "What have you learned through a painful experience?"

CHILD "What were the most important lessons you taught me when I was a baby?"

MENTOR "How can your presence help people know God better?"

CHILD "How can I feel near to God?"

CHALLENGE CHECK

How did the challenge go?
What did you learn?

WEEK 33

God so loved the world, that he gave his only Son, that whoever believes in him should not perish but have eternal life.

—JOHN 3:16

LESSON TO LEARN

God's love is so big it requires its own definition.

As our culture changes, so does our language. We still speak English, but new words are added to the dictionary every year to keep up with our changing culture. For example, the term *selfie* was added to the online Oxford dictionary in 2013 after it became a common way to describe taking a picture of oneself. Inventing words for a changing culture isn't new. It happened in the Bible too!

We use the word *love* for different things: our mom and dad, a friend, pizza, and a certain song. But those are very different kinds of love. The Bible was first written in Greek, and there are several Greek words for "love." One describes friendship and another is for romance. But John used a different Greek word for the love of God that forever changed its definition. The word is *agapē*, and it describes God's unconditional and undeserved love. It will never end, and there is nothing we can do to earn it. God changed the culture of love so much that the language of the day had to change to keep up.

Not only does God love us with undeserved love, but he wants us to demonstrate this kind of love to others as well. Loving others can be easy when people are acting lovely. But God doesn't want us to love people just when it's easy. He wants us to love with an agapē kind of love even when it's hard.

CHALLENGE

Try to memorize 1 Corinthians 13:4–7. Yes, it's hard. No, you don't have to get every word exactly right.

DAY 2

God's love is so big it requires its own definition.

MEMORY WORK

God so loved the world, that he gave his only Son, that whoever believes in him should not perish but have eternal life.
—JOHN 3:16

DAY 3

READ 1 CORINTHIANS 13:4–7.

How did God's love change the world?

How is God's love different from normal human love?

If someone doesn't know God, can they still know the love of God? How?

DAY 4

READ 1 CORINTHIANS 13:4–7 AGAIN.

What characteristic of love is easiest for you?

What characteristic of love is hardest for you?

Using this passage, talk about what love can actually look like.

Love is patient,

Example: *When my sister is copying me, I can be patient instead of yelling at her.*

love is kind.
It does not envy,
it does not boast,
it is not proud.
It does not dishonor others,
it is not self-seeking,
it is not easily angered,
it keeps no record of wrongs.
Love does not delight in evil but rejoices with the truth.
It always protects,
always trusts,
always hopes,
always perseveres. (NIV)

DAY 5

MENTORING MOMENT

MENTOR "Who is someone that you need to show more love to?"

CHILD "How has 1 Corinthians 13 helped you love someone when it wasn't easy?"

MENTOR "If Jesus's love is perfect, why isn't he loved back perfectly?"

CHILD "How should I respond when someone doesn't treat me with love?"

MENTOR "Have you ever felt unsafe with someone you were trying to love?"

CHILD "How can I show love to someone who I need boundaries with?"

CHALLENGE CHECK

How did the challenge go? What did you learn?

WEEK 34

WHAT DOES REAL WORSHIP LOOK LIKE?

God is spirit, and those who worship him
must worship in spirit and truth.

—JOHN 4:24

LESSON TO LEARN

Worship is recognizing who God
is and what he has done.

DAY 1

In a church service, *worship* most often refers to the part where we stand up and sing. Some people might even close their eyes and raise their hands. But worship isn't just about what you do with your voice or your eyes or your hands. It's about your heart! To really worship from the heart, you need to recognize that worship isn't about you at all. True worship is recognizing *who God is* and *what he has done for us.*

Who God is Have you ever heard an athlete or a celebrity give glory to God for what they just accomplished? That's not a bad thing to do. The Bible even talks about giving glory to God. When we see this phrase in the Bible, it's actually a command to recognize the glory God already has. We can't give God glory. The glory is already his. But we can recognize his glory. He created the world in six days. He parted the sea, calmed the storm, and walked on water. His power is endless, and so is his love.

What God has done for us The Bible is one long story made up of a bunch of little stories about how much God loves us. He loves us because we are his. The most important way he showed us his love was by sending his Son, Jesus, to earth to die for the sins of the world so that we can live forever in heaven with him. This is the greatest gift anyone could offer us. We don't have to earn it; we just have to accept it.

When we recognize who God is and remember what he has done for us, worship will overflow from our hearts. It will be part of everything we do and say. Your chores can be worship, the way you speak to your parents can be worship, singing in church can be worship, and the list goes on and on. When our words and our actions are full of worship, we can help others recognize God's glory.

CHALLENGE

Play a game in the car with your family. Take turns finishing this sentence: "God, what I like about you is . . ." See who comes up with the most responses.

DAY 2

Real worship is about recognizing who God is and what he has done for us.

MEMORY WORK

God is spirit, and those who worship him must worship in spirit and truth.
—JOHN 4:24

DAY 3

READ MARK 12:41–44.

 Have you ever felt like you didn't have much to offer God?

 Why was Jesus so impressed with the widow's gift?

 How can you worship God with your money?

DAY 4

READ ACTS 16:24–40.

 How did Paul and Silas teach us about true worship?

 How did Paul and Silas's worship change lives?

 How could your worship change lives?

DAY 5

MENTORING MOMENT

MENTOR "How can your activities today be worship?"

CHILD "Is there a place you feel close to God outside of church?"

MENTOR "What's your favorite way to worship God?"

CHILD "If I can worship God outside of church, why is church important?"

MENTOR "What makes our worship meaningful to God?"

CHILD "How are you tempted to make worship about you?"

CHALLENGE CHECK

How did the challenge go?
What did you learn?

WEEK 35

WHAT'S UP WITH THE SNACK DURING CHURCH?

Jesus said to them, "Truly, truly, I say to you, unless you eat the flesh of the Son of Man and drink his blood, you have no life in you."

—JOHN 6:53

LESSON TO LEARN

Communion reminds us that Jesus died for our sins and will return someday to take us to heaven.

DAY 1

The Fourth of July has been an official holiday since 1870. But our country has been celebrating the beginning of the United States of America since 1776. We remember the birth of our country with festivals, fireworks, food, music, parades, and gatherings with friends and family. All these things serve as physical reminders of where we have been and inspiration for where we will go.

Jesus gave us a very important physical reminder too. The night before he died, he celebrated the Passover with his disciples. The Passover was a ceremonial meal designed to help the Israelites remember that God had kept his promise to rescue them from slavery in Egypt. During this particular Passover, Jesus asked his disciples to remember something else too. He gave his disciples bread to remember his body, broken for them, and wine to remember his blood, poured out to cover the sins of the world. Churches still do this today. We call it communion or the Lord's Supper. When we take communion, we should remember that Jesus came to save us from our sins, but we should also remember that he is coming again.

Communion helps us remember the past. We can still remember that God was faithful to his people and delivered them from slavery. We can also remember that Jesus died to deliver us from being slaves to our sin.

Communion helps us remember the future. Just like the Passover reminded the Jews of God's faithfulness, communion can remind us of God's promise that he is going to return. He has promised a place in heaven to those who make him king of their hearts.

CHALLENGE

Have a communion celebration in your home around a full meal. You could use a special loaf of bread and juice, or you could use anything you have on hand.

DAY 2

Communion reminds us that Jesus died for our sins and will return someday to take us to heaven.

MEMORY WORK

Jesus said to them, "Truly, truly, I say to you, unless you eat the flesh of the Son of Man and drink his blood, you have no life in you."
—JOHN 6:53

DAY 3

READ EXODUS 12.

What do the bread and juice of communion represent?

Why is it important to remember the meaning of communion?

How is Jesus's death foreshadowed in the other elements of the Passover story: lamb, firstborn son, blood?

DAY 4

READ LUKE 22:14–20.

What is Jesus asking us to remember when we take communion?

Are there other symbols or actions in church that remind us of Jesus's sacrifice?

Do you have things at home or at school that help you remember Jesus?

DAY 5

MENTORING MOMENT

MENTOR "What's the most memorable meal you've ever had? Why?"

CHILD "Are there things you put on the table at special meals to remember something you love?"

MENTOR "What are some things we do besides meals that help us celebrate and remember things?"

CHILD "What does the Lord's Supper mean to you?"

MENTOR "How are baptism and the Lord's Supper similar in how they remind us of Jesus?"

CHILD "How is the Lord's Supper practiced in different churches?"

CHALLENGE CHECK

How did the challenge go? What did you learn?

WEEK 36

CAN I KNOW I'M SAVED?

I give them eternal life, and they will never perish, and no one will snatch them out of my hand.

—JOHN 10:28

LESSON TO LEARN

God will never let you go or let you down.

DAY 1

Bullying is a problem in many schools. But do you know who is never bullied? The kid standing right next to the principal! The same is true in our spiritual lives. As long as we are standing next to God, Satan can't bully us, no one can snatch us away from God, and not even the worst circumstances in our lives can destroy our faith. Why? Because God is faithful to us.

Read our memory verse for this week again. That is a powerful promise you need to hold on to when things get tough.

On the other hand, other verses suggest that someone could choose to walk away from God. John 15:6 says, "If anyone does not abide in me he is thrown away like a branch and withers; and the branches are gathered, thrown into the fire, and burned." We are secure in God's presence, but we can't take that presence for granted. The Bible teaches us to be faithful to God just as he is faithful to us.

So, are Christians secure in their salvation? Absolutely! The Bible promises that we are always loved and protected by God. *No one* can pull you away from God. But the Bible also suggests that some people choose to turn their backs on God. The Bible warns us not to abandon or neglect our relationship with God. God's biggest concern is our hearts. He wants our hearts to be his from the moment we confess him as our savior until we get to be with him in heaven. Will we continue to sin after giving our lives to Jesus? Of course we will. We're human. But we can't let forgiveness give us permission to sin. When our hearts belong to God, we desire to do things his way.

CHALLENGE

Do nothing . . . because that's what you have to do to earn God's love.

DAY 2

God will never let go of you. Cling to him with the same intensity that he clings to you.

MEMORY WORK

I give them eternal life, and they will never perish, and no one will snatch them out of my hand.
—JOHN 10:28

DAY 3

READ JOHN 6:22–40.

 What did Jesus say his job is?

 What does Jesus's job teach us about our job as Christians on earth?

 Why is God the only one who can judge our hearts?

DAY 4

READ HEBREWS 6:1–12.

 What does it mean to fall away from God?

 What's the difference between sinning and rejecting God?

 How can you protect yourself from rejecting (or abandoning) God?

DAY 5

MENTORING MOMENT

MENTOR "How is God protecting you now?"

CHILD "What do you do to keep me safe?"

MENTOR "Is there a way you can run from God's protection?"

CHILD "If God is protecting me, does that mean bad things won't happen to me?"

MENTOR "Do you know anyone who acts like a Christian at church but not at school? Why is that dangerous?"

CHILD "Have you known someone who rejected God after living as a Christian? What happened?"

CHALLENGE CHECK

How did the challenge go?
What did you learn?

WEEK 37

WHAT DOES THE HOLY SPIRIT DO FOR ME?

You will receive power when the Holy Spirit has come upon you, and you will be my witnesses in Jerusalem and in all Judea and Samaria, and to the end of the earth.

—ACTS 1:8

LESSON TO LEARN

The Holy Spirit is God's voice inside us.

DAY 1

Have you ever wondered how people hear the voice of God? Samuel heard God calling his name in the night (1 Samuel 3). He thought it was Eli, the priest, calling him, but it was actually God. Sometimes God speaks to people in an audible voice, sometimes God speaks through other people, but a lot of the time, God chooses to speak to people through the Holy Spirit in their hearts.

The Holy Spirit is the Spirit of God. When Christians decide to follow and serve God, God gives them the gift of the Holy Spirit. He lives in you. He can speak audibly to you, but more often he provides you with a certain gut instinct that has nothing to do with your gut. Have you ever had a friend or family member on your mind all day and later found out that the person was sick or sad? That was probably the Holy Spirit speaking to you. Have you ever been on the playground and felt a nudge to talk to the kid playing all alone? That was probably the Holy Spirit speaking to you. Have you ever been moved by a song or a sermon? That was probably the Holy Spirit speaking to you.

The Holy Spirit transforms our lives from the inside out. He convicts us when we sin. He encourages us when we're sad. He gives us the right words to speak to others about Jesus. And if we let him, he strengthens us to do the right thing so we can look and act more like Jesus. When we let him work *in* us, he can also work *through* us to help point others to the love of God.

CHALLENGE

Spend a few minutes each day alone in a quiet space. Ask God to be near to you in the silence.

DAY 2

The Holy Spirit is God's voice inside us, and he can transform our lives.

MEMORY WORK

You will receive power when the Holy Spirit has come upon you, and you will be my witnesses in Jerusalem and in all Judea and Samaria, and to the end of the earth.
—ACTS 1:8

DAY 3

READ ACTS 2:1–13.

If you were to witness a miracle, what do you think you would like to see?

What's it like to be around someone who is full of the Holy Spirit?

Have you ever felt like the Holy Spirit spoke to you or gave you the power to do something?

DAY 4

READ ACTS 2:14–41.

Why did so many people decide to get baptized that day?

Why did this miracle convince so many people that Peter was telling the truth about Jesus?

What about your life would convince people you were telling the truth about Jesus?

DAY 5

MENTORING MOMENT

MENTOR "Be very, very quiet for thirty seconds. Listen for sounds you've never paid attention to before. What did you hear?"

CHILD "Have you ever heard God speak to you? Was it audible or more like a gut feeling?"

MENTOR "Can God be speaking even if we aren't hearing him?"

CHILD "How can you know it's God talking to you?"

MENTOR "How can we make sure we're listening for the Holy Spirit's voice?"

CHILD "How has the Holy Spirit in your heart changed your life?"

CHALLENGE CHECK

How did the challenge go? What did you learn?

WEEK 38

WHY DID JESUS LEAVE THE EARTH?

When he had said these things, as they were looking on, he was lifted up, and a cloud took him out of their sight.

—ACTS 1:9

LESSON TO LEARN

We complete Jesus's mission with the help of his Spirit.

DAY 1

What goes up must come down, right? But in Jesus's case, what comes down must go up. Jesus was in heaven before he came to earth. He had been sent on a special mission to save the world. Once his mission was complete, he floated back to heaven. This is called the Ascension. Sounds a bit wild, doesn't it? But Jesus often did things that defied the laws of nature. After all, we're talking about the same Jesus who walked on water, brought people back to life, calmed the sea, and fed a crowd of five thousand people with five loaves of bread and two fish. The Ascension was his final act on earth that proved he was God. It's also super important because it proved he completed his mission.

That's why, right before Jesus ascended, he passed the baton to us. Now we have a special mission too! Our mission is to carry on what Jesus started—to tell the world who Jesus is and how much he loves them. The coolest part of God's plan is, even though Jesus is no longer physically on earth, he's actually more with us now than he ever was. You see, when he left, the Holy Spirit came in his place. (Remember that from last week?) Jesus gave us a mission, and he also gave us the Holy Spirit to help us complete it! It's like when you learned to ride your bike without training wheels. Maybe your mom or dad ran beside your bike, holding on to your seat. You were nervous, but you still had the comfort of knowing someone was there. But then your mom or dad let go. It might have been terrifying at first, but then you realized that you could ride a bike without anyone holding on. When Jesus ascended into heaven, he was letting go of the bike. But the Spirit is still right beside us, helping us go further and faster than we ever thought possible.

CHALLENGE

Pay attention to the Spirit's prompting this week. When you feel prompted to serve or encourage someone (even if you don't know the person), do it! (But make sure to follow your parents' rules about talking to strangers.)

DAY 2

Jesus's mission was to die for the sins of the world and rise again. When Jesus left the earth, he left his Spirit in our hearts. Now our mission is to make him famous by sharing his love with the world.

MEMORY WORK

When he had said these things, as they were looking on, he was lifted up, and a cloud took him out of their sight.
—ACTS 1:9

DAY 3

READ ACTS 1:1-11.

Why did Jesus leave the earth?

What is Jesus doing for us now?

What can we do to continue Jesus's mission on earth?

DAY 4

READ JOHN 16:7-16.

How does the Spirit help us?

What does the Holy Spirit do to help us carry out Jesus's mission on earth?

Has the Spirit ever convicted you of sin?

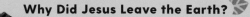

DAY 5

MENTORING MOMENT

MENTOR "What do you think is easier for God to use: your talents or your willingness?"

CHILD "Has the Spirit ever helped you accomplish something Jesus wanted you to do?"

MENTOR "What hinders your willingness to partner with Jesus in his mission?"

CHILD "What have you done that has increased your willingness?"

MENTOR "How can your gifts/talents work together with other people's gifts/talents to share God's love with the world?"

CHILD "How do you see me using my gifts for God now? When I'm an adult?"

CHALLENGE CHECK

How did the challenge go?
What did you learn?

WEEK 39

WHY SHOULD I BE BAPTIZED?

Repent and be baptized every one of you in the name of Jesus Christ for the forgiveness of your sins, and you will receive the gift of the Holy Spirit.

—ACTS 2:38

LESSON TO LEARN

Baptism is imitating Jesus's death and promising to live for him.

DAY 1

Do you want to know a secret? The water in the baptistry at church isn't special. That's right! No secret sauce, no pixie dust, no special potion. The power of baptism comes from heaven, not your faucet. You could get baptized in a river, a pool, the ocean, or even a bathtub. It's not about the water. It's about what the water represents.

Baptism is a reenactment of what Jesus did for us through his death, burial, and resurrection. When you go under the water, you're saying to Jesus, "You died and were buried for me, so I am going to die to myself and make you my Lord." When you come up out of the water, you're showing that you receive the gift of God's Holy Spirit to lead and guide you in your new life.

Death The Bible tells us we can't serve two masters (Matthew 6:24). If God isn't our king, something or someone else will be. Just as Jesus died for our sins, we must put to death our other masters so we can serve God. This is a symbolic death. If money is your master, tithing the first 10 percent of your allowance could help keep God on his throne in your heart. If sports are your master, not allowing yourself to play, watch, or read about sports until you've spent time reading your Bible and praying could help keep God on his throne in your heart. Baptism won't make God king of your heart, but it shows the rest of the world that you want him to be.

Burial Being submerged under the water represents the burial of Jesus. When a casket is buried in the ground, it's permanent. Digging it back up takes special permission. Unfortunately, sin is a little more complicated. Sin tends to sneak back up to the surface. It needs to be buried over and over. This doesn't mean that we need to be baptized over and over. We just need to keep putting God back on his throne as king of our hearts.

Resurrection Just as Jesus rose again, we rise up out of the water to start a

CHALLENGE

Drink only water this week as a sacrificial reminder that it's not the water that's special but our hearts.

new life. Have you ever heard the term *born again*? We don't actually start our lives over as babies. But we start a new life with God as king of our hearts and live the rest of our days making him famous.

DAY 2

Baptism is imitating Jesus's death and promising to live for him.

MEMORY WORK

Repent and be baptized every one of you in the name of Jesus Christ for the forgiveness of your sins, and you will receive the gift of the Holy Spirit.
—ACTS 2:38

DAY 3

READ ROMANS 6:1–6.

 What does baptism represent?

 Is baptism for people who have recently believed in Jesus, or is it for people who are already mature in their faith?

 What does it mean to die to yourself?

DAY 4

READ MATTHEW 4:1–11.

 What was Jesus's weapon against temptation?

 After Jesus was baptized, Satan tempted him. Do you think Satan will tempt you more when you're obeying God or when you're disobeying God? Why?

 How can you prepare yourself now for when you're tempted?

DAY 5

MENTORING MOMENT

MENTOR "Imitating someone means copying them because you think that person is really great. Whom have you imitated?"

CHILD "How is baptism imitating Jesus?"

MENTOR "How are you imitating Jesus?"

CHILD "How do you put God back on the throne of your heart after you sin?"

MENTOR "Is there someone you need to stop imitating?"

CHILD "Does Jesus still love you if you're not baptized?"

CHALLENGE CHECK

How did the challenge go? What did you learn?

WEEK 40

WHAT IS GOD'S SOLUTION TO RACISM?

[God] made from one man every nation of mankind to live on all the face of the earth, having determined allotted periods and the boundaries of their dwelling place.

—ACTS 17:26

LESSON TO LEARN

All people have equal worth in God's eyes.

DAY 1

Most of us are familiar with names like Rosa Parks and Martin Luther King Jr. There is even a national holiday to remember and celebrate what Martin Luther King Jr. spent his life doing: fighting racism. Racism, as Dr. King experienced it, was White people mistreating Black people simply because they were Black. America has made some big strides against racism since Dr. King's day. But the truth is that racism still exists. And it's not limited to Black and White. Racism happens all over the world, and it was a reality for people in Bible times too. A quick internet search will show you endless resources about racism—different opinions about it, how to handle it, and how to talk about it. Some resources even contradict one another. Fortunately, God has given us the ultimate resource: the Bible. When there are tricky questions about life, it's always best to ask, "What does God say about this in the Bible?"

So, What *Does* God Say About Racism?

God created man in his own image.
—GENESIS 1:27

[God] made from one man every nation of mankind.
—ACTS 17:26

You created my inmost being;
you knit me together in my mother's womb.
I praise you because I am fearfully and wonderfully made;
your works are wonderful.
—PSALM 139:13–14, NIV

What Does This Mean?

God created all humans in his image. Humans are his favorite part of creation. He created us and said we were *very* good. Inside all of us, God places gifts, talents, and qualities that reveal his majesty. He gave us the land and animals to rule over, but he never asked people to rule over other people.

God designed us on purpose. He didn't accidently come up with different people groups. He designed humanity that way. If you've ever built a challenging Lego set, you might understand the feeling. You very carefully searched for just the right piece to put in just the right place. You might even still have this creation on display because you're so proud of it. Can you imagine if someone broke it apart? God, our Creator, feels the same about us. He wants all his creation to be respected and appreciated.

CHALLENGE

When you encounter someone who seems different, practice saying in your mind, *This person is a special child of God*, in order to see them the way God does.

DAY 2

God's solution to racism is to treat every human being as a precious child of God.

MEMORY WORK

[God] made from one man every nation of mankind to live on all the face of the earth, having determined allotted periods and the boundaries of their dwelling place.
—ACTS 17:26

DAY 3

READ JONAH 1.
Before you read, remember that Jonah didn't want to go to preach to the people of Nineveh. He grew up disliking them because they disrespected God. Jonah didn't want to preach to them because he didn't want them to have the opportunity to know God.

 Why was Jonah hiding from God?

 Why was God upset by Jonah's actions?

 Is there anyone you need to share God's love with even if you feel like they don't deserve it?

DAY 4

READ PSALM 139:13–16.

 How would this make you feel if God wrote this to *you*?

 How would this make you feel if God wrote this to someone you have a hard time getting along with? What does this reveal about your heart?

 Why is it hard to offer grace to others? Why is it hard to offer grace to yourself?

DAY 5

MENTORING MOMENT

MENTOR "Have you ever ignored an adult when they asked you to do something you didn't want to do?"

CHILD "How is ignoring God similar to and different from ignoring an adult?"

MENTOR "Have you seen anyone getting picked on at school? How would God want you to treat that person?"

CHILD "How should I treat a person who mistreats others?"

MENTOR "Have you ever refused to include someone because you didn't like them or were upset with them?"

CHILD "Have you ever rejected someone because of their character or some other characteristic?"

CHALLENGE CHECK

How did the challenge go?
What did you learn?

WEEK 41

There is therefore now no condemnation
for those who are in Christ Jesus.

—ROMANS 8:1

LESSON TO LEARN

Jesus completely frees us from guilt and shame.

DAY 1

In third grade, I kept a secret from my parents: I had a boyfriend at school. I knew I wasn't supposed to, so after three days I sent my friends to break up with him for me. (For the record, this isn't how dating is supposed to happen.) I felt so guilty, and I didn't want my parents to be upset with me, so I kept it a secret. I thought about it way more than was normal. I was constantly nervous that my parents would find out and be disappointed in me. Months went by, and I was still thinking about how upset my parents would be if they only knew the truth. One day my mom randomly asked me whether I had ever had a boyfriend. I thought she must have found out my secret, and I broke down sobbing. After I confessed to her and we talked about it, I never really thought about it again. With her forgiveness, I was free from the guilt and shame of disobeying my parents. It no longer consumed my heart and mind.

This is the kind of freedom that God offers to us. He never wants us to feel alone, trapped by our sins, or unworthy of his love. He gave Adam and Eve a perfect garden, where they were in perfect harmony with him and all his creation. We know what happened next. Sin wrecked God's plan for our freedom. But that couldn't stop his love. God made another way. Jesus became the final sacrifice for our sins. No matter how big, small, public, or private your sins are, Jesus says, "I took care of that. I forgive you." When we truly accept his forgiveness, we will free up places in our hearts and minds where guilt and shame don't belong. Although you may feel like a sinner, God wants you to know that you're his child. He wants to offer you his forgiveness and the freedom that comes from accepting that.

CHALLENGE

Write down a list of sins that you've committed or that have been committed against you. Now destroy the paper. Ask God to help your heart move on.

DAY 2

Accepting God's free gift of forgiveness brings freedom.

MEMORY WORK

There is therefore now no condemnation for those who are in Christ Jesus.
—ROMANS 8:1

DAY 3

READ JOHN 8:1–11.

 Why did everyone drop their rocks?

 Are there ways we hurt people today with words rather than rocks?

 Have you ever felt like the woman in this story?

DAY 4

READ ROMANS 8:1–11.

 What is condemnation? How does Jesus make it disappear?

 Why is there freedom when you accept forgiveness?

 Is it harder to forgive yourself or others? Why?

DAY 5

MENTORING MOMENT

MENTOR "Are you carrying around any guilt? What would help you let it go?"

CHILD "Was there ever a time that you carried guilt around longer than you should? What helped you let it go?"

MENTOR "Are you withholding forgiveness from someone? What would help you forgive?"

CHILD "What do I do if I forgive someone but then anger takes over again?"

MENTOR "The saying goes, 'Forgive and forget.' But should things always go back to normal after you've forgiven someone?"

CHILD "What do I do if someone won't forgive me?"

CHALLENGE CHECK

How did the challenge go? What did you learn?

WEEK 42

Do not be conformed to this world, but be transformed by the renewal of your mind, that by testing you may discern what is the will of God, what is good and acceptable and perfect.

—ROMANS 12:2

LESSON TO LEARN

God has given you everything you need to transform your life.

DAY 1

"Show me your friends, and I'll show you your future." Have you ever heard this saying? It's true. We act most like those we like best. If your friends are working hard in school, honoring their parents, and achieving their goals, you'll be more likely to do those things too. But it's also true that if your friends are disrespecting their parents, using inappropriate language, and cheating on tests, you'll be more likely to do *those* things. When you're faced with a decision between right and wrong, you have two choices. You can conform or you can be transformed. When you conform to the world, you imitate the world's behaviors. But when you're transformed by Jesus, you act like Jesus.

Here are some godly tools for transformation:

1. **The Bible** is full of wisdom and real-life stories that can help guide all your decisions. If you ever wonder what Jesus would do, just open your Bible and you'll get your answer.
2. **Worship music** focuses your mind on God. If you don't believe this one, you can test it. Play some worship music, and observe the changes in your attitude. When we lift up our praises to God, our attitudes are lifted up as well.
3. **Service.** Jesus lived his life in service to others. When we do the same, we get to know him better.
4. **Church.** God wants you to meet with people who will encourage and inspire you to continue this life of transformation.

CHALLENGE

Choose at least one transformation tool to use each day this week.

DAY 2

We can change by using the tools God has given us: the Bible, worship music, service, and church.

MEMORY WORK

Do not be conformed to this world, but be transformed by the renewal of your mind, that by testing you may discern what is the will of God, what is good and acceptable and perfect.
—ROMANS 12:2

DAY 3

READ MATTHEW 17:1–13.

Jesus wasn't just transformed; he was transfigured. What do you think the difference is?

How is your life more beautiful when it's transformed?

Which transformation tool has been most helpful in transforming your life?

DAY 4

READ MATTHEW 17:14–20.

How did God transform this boy's life?

Have you ever seen or heard about something that seemed impossible but happened with God's help?

How can God help you transform your life, even if you feel like it's impossible?

DAY 5

MENTORING MOMENT

MENTOR "Which transformation tool are you least comfortable with? How can I help you become more comfortable with that?"

CHILD "When my life is transformed, will you be able to tell by looking at me?"

MENTOR "What habit or attitude would you like to change to look more like Jesus?"

CHILD "What steps can I take to make that change?"

MENTOR "In what situations do you find yourself conforming the most?"

CHILD "How have your friendships affected your life?"

CHALLENGE CHECK

How did the challenge go?
What did you learn?

WEEK 43

HOW CAN I KNOW GOD'S WILL FOR MY LIFE?

"Who has understood the mind of the Lord so as to instruct him?" But we have the mind of Christ.

—1 CORINTHIANS 2:16

LESSON TO LEARN

God wants you to know and follow his will for your life.

DAY 1

In the nineties, it was popular to wear bracelets with the letters *WWJD* on them. That stands for "What would Jesus do?" Although it became a fashion statement, it began as a reminder to act and react like Jesus would. The Bible helps us understand not only what Jesus would do but also what God wants us to do. That's right! We *can* know God's will for our lives.

God has two kinds of will: general and specific. In general, God wants the same thing for all of us. He wants us to be saved: "[God] is patient with you, not wanting anyone to perish, but everyone to come to repentance" (2 Peter 3:9, NIV). But he has a specific will for your life too. His specific will for you will look different from his will for your friends. Can you imagine if God's specific will for everyone was to be a teacher? Who would we go to when we got sick? Would we still have songs to listen to? Would we still have sports to play or watch on TV? God designed us each uniquely, and he also has unique plans for each of our lives.

Knowing God's specific will for your life is possible. The Bible won't say, "I want you to be a doctor or teacher." But it does say, "We have received not the spirit of the world, but the Spirit who is from God, that we might understand the things freely given us by God. And we impart this in words not taught by human wisdom but taught by the Spirit, interpreting spiritual truths to those who are spiritual. . . . "'Who has understood the mind of the Lord so as to instruct him?' But we have the mind of Christ" (1 Corinthians 2:12–13, 16). God has given us parents, teachers, coaches, and counselors to help us see God's will for us and his nature in us. But most importantly, God has given us his Spirit to help us think and act like he would.

The Spirit of God in you is a powerful tool and should be taken very seriously because when he isn't, you lose your ability to fully know God's will. If you don't think that's possible, sit quietly in your house for a few minutes. Did a car drive by? Did the air conditioner turn on?

Did the ice maker in the freezer dump ice? You've grown so used to sounds in your house that you don't even really hear them anymore. We can grow used to ignoring God's Spirit in us too. The longer you continue behavior that God wants you to turn from, the harder it will be to recognize that it's not God's will for your life. When you feel God's Spirit prompting you to follow his will, follow it! The more you practice listening to the Spirit, the more you will hear him speak.

CHALLENGE

Sit outside for five minutes, and pay attention to everything you see, hear, smell, and feel. See how many things you can notice when you're tuned in to them.

DAY 2

Ultimately, God wants everyone to be saved. You can share his love wherever you are and whatever you're doing.

MEMORY WORK

"Who has understood the mind of the Lord so as to instruct him?" But we have the mind of Christ.
—1 CORINTHIANS 2:16

DAY 3

READ 1 SAMUEL 3:1–19.

Why do you think God chose to speak to Samuel rather than Eli?

What does God's voice sound or feel like?

How can you protect yourself from tuning out God's voice?

DAY 4

READ JOHN 7:14–18.

Why were people so amazed at Jesus's teaching?

What would it look like for someone to have the mind of Christ?

Are there influences keeping you from having the mind of Christ?

DAY 5

MENTORING MOMENT

MENTOR "Have you ever felt God's Spirit nudging you?"

CHILD "What kinds of things will God say to me when he speaks?"

MENTOR "How are you listening for God's voice?"

CHILD "What are some ways you see that I might be in danger of tuning out God's voice?"

MENTOR "How can you follow God's general plan for your life today?"

CHILD "Do I have to know God's specific plan for my life right now?"

CHALLENGE CHECK

How did the challenge go? What did you learn?

WEEK 44

DID JESUS REALLY RISE FROM THE DEAD?

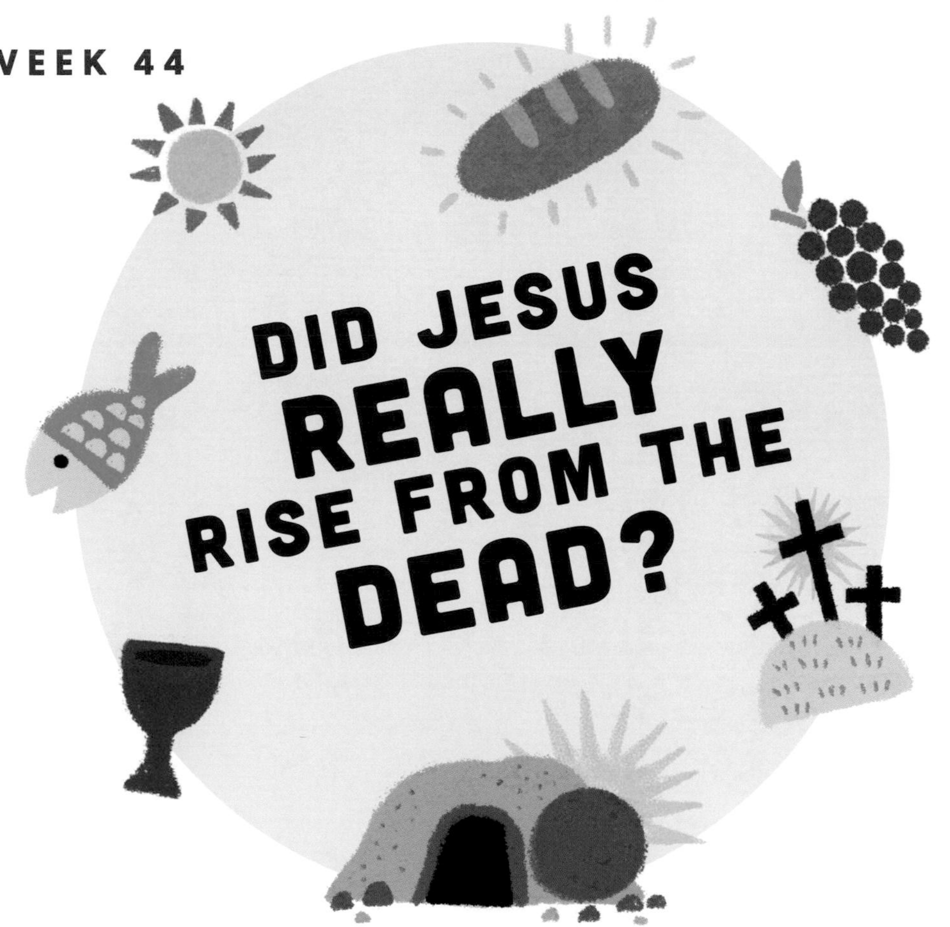

If Christ has not been raised, then our preaching is in vain and your faith is in vain.

—1 CORINTHIANS 15:14

LESSON TO LEARN

Jesus's resurrection is the core of Christianity.

DAY 1

Jesus did many things that seem impossible. He healed people who couldn't walk or see. He even brought dead people back to life. His own death and resurrection are especially hard to make sense of.

Jesus was crucified. There's no debate about that. This information is found in the Bible and in writings by people who didn't believe in Jesus. Soldiers guarded his tomb day and night so that no one could steal his body. If the soldiers had allowed anything to happen to his body, they would have lost their own lives. But something *did* happen to Jesus's body. When Mary and Mary Magdalene went to visit the tomb on the third day, it was empty. After the women discovered the empty tomb, people began seeing Jesus face to face. This is why Christians believe that Jesus rose from the dead. It's the core of Christianity.

Here's why it matters to us:

Jesus's death gave us forgiveness from our sins; his resurrection gives us hope for eternity. He's alive! He promised he's coming again. Only next time, he's taking us back to heaven with him!

Jesus ascended back to heaven to sit at the right hand of the throne of God. He is now enthroned as king of the world.

Jesus defends us before the Father. When we sin, Jesus opens his hands, shows God his wounds, and says, "I paid for that."

We now have the power of the Holy Spirit. When Jesus ascended into heaven, the Holy Spirit was sent to live inside our hearts to guide our thoughts, words, and actions.

The Resurrection isn't just some random historical fact we believe. It gives us real power to live differently today. We can face any challenge, knowing that we are forgiven of our sins and will live eternally because of what Jesus did. And someday, just as he was resurrected, we will be resurrected too.

CHALLENGE

Write down your questions about the Bible or your faith. Ask a mentor to help you find answers.

DAY 2

Jesus's resurrection is historically true and the core of Christianity.

MEMORY WORK

If Christ has not been raised, then our preaching is in vain and your faith is in vain.
—1 CORINTHIANS 15:14

DAY 3

READ MARK 16:1–13.

 Why was it hard for people to believe that Jesus had risen?

 In this story, what helped people come to believe Jesus rose?

 Why is it so important that Jesus rose from the dead?

DAY 4

READ MARK 16:14–20.

 Why did Jesus rebuke his disciples?

 Did the disciples' unbelief change the fact that Jesus was alive?

 If you really believed Jesus rose from the dead, what else could you trust him with?

DAY 5

MENTORING MOMENT

MENTOR "What would help you believe that someone's story was true?"

CHILD "Would you risk your life to tell a lie? What about the truth?"

MENTOR "Why should you believe the disciples' testimony that Jesus rose from the dead?"

CHILD "Is it okay to have questions about things we read in the Bible?"

MENTOR "What's the hardest part about believing in Jesus?"

CHILD "Why do you believe that Jesus rose from the dead?"

CHALLENGE CHECK

How did the challenge go? What did you learn?

WEEK 45

WHAT DO I HAVE TO DO TO BE SAVED?

By grace you have been saved through faith.
And this is not your own doing; it is the gift of God.

—EPHESIANS 2:8

LESSON TO LEARN

Good works are a result of receiving God's grace.

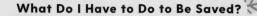

DAY 1

When your dad asks you to hang up the phone, you know what he means—end the call. Ending a call today usually means touching a red circle on a screen. But phones used to be attached to the wall, and when people finished talking, they had to hang the pieces of the phone back on the wall. This term *hang up* is still used even though the picture in our minds of hanging up is different.

The word *grace* in the Bible is a good example of this.

Ephesians 2:8–10 says, "By grace you have been saved through faith. And this is not your own doing; it is the gift of God, not a result of works, so that no one may boast. For we are his workmanship, created in Christ Jesus for good works, which God prepared beforehand, that we should walk in them." We are saved by grace and created for good works. Let's look at history to help us understand.

Today we divide society into levels of wealth (upper class, middle class, lower class). Society in Bible times was also divided, but they had different names and different expectations for each group.

Patrons This group of people had most of the money and most of the power. They hired lower classes to do jobs for them, and they provided for every need of their workers. The gifts that patrons gave to meet their workers' needs were called *grace*.

Clients This group of people were poor workers. They relied on their patrons to meet their needs. In return, they helped with whatever the patrons wanted. The loyalty the clients gave their patrons in exchange for meeting their needs was called *faith*.

Our words *grace* and *faith* are demonstrated perfectly in this social system. When we receive God's grace, we owe him our faith. Faith isn't a way to earn grace. It's a result of it. We are faithful to God because of his gift of grace to us.

Read Ephesians 2:8 again with this knowledge.

CHALLENGE

This week, show grace to someone who doesn't deserve it and gratitude to someone who does.

DAY 2

When you accept Jesus, good works will be the natural result of receiving God's grace.

MEMORY WORK

By grace you have been saved through faith. And this is not your own doing; it is the gift of God.
—EPHESIANS 2:8

DAY 3

READ LUKE 15:1-10.

God cares about your soul the same way the shepherd cares about his lost sheep and the same way the woman cares about her lost coin. How does that make you feel?

What do these parts of the stories represent?
lost sheep
shepherd
lost coin
woman

How is God like a patron? How are you like a client?

DAY 4

READ LUKE 15:11-32.

What changed in the son to make him return home?

What do these parts of the story represent?
younger son
father
older son
pigsty

How does this story remind you of your relationship with God?

DAY 5

MENTORING MOMENT

MENTOR "What's the most important item you've ever lost and found? How did you feel when you found it?"

CHILD "Is that how God feels when he finds us?"

MENTOR "What makes you part of our family? What are things you do because you're part of our family?"

CHILD "How would you feel if you lost me? Is that how God would feel?"

MENTOR "With your new understanding of faith and grace, what does our memory verse mean?"

CHILD "Are there areas of my life where my actions don't reflect my belief in God's grace?"

CHALLENGE CHECK

How did the challenge go? What did you learn?

HOW CAN I HELP THE CHURCH?

There is one body and one Spirit—just as you were called to the one hope that belongs to your call—one Lord, one faith, one baptism, one God and Father of all, who is over all and through all and in all. But grace was given to each one of us according to the measure of Christ's gift.

—EPHESIANS 4:4–7

LESSON TO LEARN

God has gifted you with power to change the world.

DAY 1

If you're like me, when you see a bee, you probably reach for the closest thing to swat it away with. But these buzzing creatures are amazing and super important to the earth. There are actually three types of bees within a hive, and each has a specific job. The queen bee's job is to lay eggs. The worker bees have several jobs, but one of the most important is to leave the hive to find pollen. The drone bees have only one job: reproduction. A colony of bees works together in such an impressive way. They all need one another for their colony to function properly. If one type of bee decided to quit their job, the whole colony would fall apart.

God created the church to be unified, just like a colony of bees. The Bible calls our jobs "spiritual gifts." There are lots of different spiritual gifts, but they all have the same purpose—to serve the whole church. Each person has a special ability that contributes to the health of the church.

Gifts are for giving to other people. Spiritual gifts are no different. They are abilities that you already have that you can use to serve others. For example, if you're a talented baker, you could bake cookies for your new neighbor. If you're really outgoing, you could invite someone to come play with you at recess. Sometimes spiritual gifts feel like they're made for adults. But spiritual gifts are for kids too! And figuring out what *your* spiritual gift is doesn't have to be that hard. Let's make it simple: Walk into a room; find what needs to be done that you would be good at; do it. That's your spiritual gift.

The bee colony would collapse without each bee doing its job. And the church would collapse without each Christian exercising their spiritual gift for the good of the whole. When we all do our part, our gifts work together to make Jesus famous.

CHALLENGE

Write a short story or poem about a hand that took over the job of the head.

DAY 2

God has given each Christian a spiritual gift. Together our gifts can change the world.

MEMORY WORK

There is one body and one Spirit—just as you were called to the one hope that belongs to your call.
—EPHESIANS 4:4

DAY 3

READ 1 CORINTHIANS 12:12-27.

How is the church body like a human body?

What abilities do you have? How do they make your class, team, or family better?

What could happen in your family or church if you stopped using your talents?

DAY 4

READ EPHESIANS 4:11-16.

Who is the head of the church body? How should we treat him?

What would happen if a different body part tried to be the head?

What's an example of how one spiritual gift could complement a different spiritual gift of another person? Example: Sawyer doesn't know much about the Bible, but he's popular because he's a football star. He can invite his friends to church because his pastor does know a lot about the Bible.

DAY 5

MENTORING MOMENT

MENTOR “What abilities or characteristics do you have that no one else in our family has?”

CHILD “What are ways I could improve my abilities? Do I need to if they are gifts?”

MENTOR “Have you ever wished you had different gifts?”

CHILD “Is it okay to still try to be good at things that aren’t as natural for me?”

MENTOR “How can you make sure you’re keeping Jesus as the head?”

CHILD “How have you handled situations where you wanted to play a different role?”

CHALLENGE CHECK

How did the challenge go?
What did you learn?

WEEK 47

WHY IS HUMILITY IMPORTANT?

Have this mind among yourselves, which is yours in Christ Jesus, who, though he was in the form of God, did not count equality with God a thing to be grasped, but emptied himself, by taking the form of a servant, being born in the likeness of men.

—PHILIPPIANS 2:5–7

LESSON TO LEARN

Humility will make you great.

DAY 1

Prom. Girls prepare for it weeks in advance and spend hours getting ready on the day itself. They choose the perfect dress, plan exactly how they'll wear their hair, and wait excitedly for their chance to be a princess. But that's not what Bekah did. Instead, Bekah made plans for two students with disabilities from her school. She made sure they had pretty clothes, perfect hair, a fun ride, and even a fancy dinner. Instead of focusing on herself, Bekah focused on making the night an extra special experience for others. Stories like these inspire us because people living lives of humility are rare.

A lot of people think that humility is thinking less of yourself. "I'm not that good." "She's a better artist than I am." "I can't take credit. He did the work too." It's good to give credit where credit is due. But thinking less of yourself is false humility. One book, *This Was Your Life!* by Rick Howard and Jamie Lash, puts it perfectly: "Real humility is not thinking less of ourselves; it is thinking of ourselves less."

When you think of yourself less, it leaves more room to think of others. There's another saying that you've probably heard before: "Actions speak louder than words." Doing what your sibling wants to do, picking up a mess that you didn't make, giving up a seat for someone else—these are all ways that your actions can speak louder than your words.

Jesus's actions spoke louder than his words. He gave up heaven, was born to poor parents, and loved people that the rest of society didn't care about. He took on our punishment so we could have the gift of God's grace. He lived his whole life for the benefit of others, and he calls us to do the same. Ultimately, Jesus took his place next to God on the throne. Through his humility, God was able to exalt him. This is true of our lives too. When we look for ways to serve others, God looks for ways to lift us up.

CHALLENGE

For one hour this week, pretend that you're your mom's servant . . . but don't tell her when you're doing it.

DAY 2

When we look for ways to serve others, God looks for ways to lift us up.

MEMORY WORK

Have this mind among yourselves, which is yours in Christ Jesus, who, though he was in the form of God, did not count equality with God a thing to be grasped, but emptied himself, by taking the form of a servant, being born in the likeness of men.

—PHILIPPIANS 2:5–7

DAY 3

READ GENESIS 37:3-11, 20-28.

Joseph could have taken his revenge on his brothers for selling him into slavery. Why didn't he?

When have you taken revenge instead of living humbly?

Why is humility more effective than revenge?

DAY 4

READ GENESIS 41:46-49, 53-57.

How did God lift Joseph up because of his decision to live humbly even when resources were plentiful?

Why is it hard for us to live humbly?

How can you live humbly even when resources are plentiful?

DAY 5

MENTORING MOMENT

MENTOR "What's one way you can serve others today?"

CHILD "What's the hardest part of humility?"

MENTOR "When has someone treated you with humility?"

CHILD "What do I do when someone doesn't treat me with humility?"

MENTOR "Is it okay to admit when you're good at something?"

CHILD "What's a gift you see in me? How does it bless others?"

CHALLENGE CHECK

How did the challenge go? What did you learn?

WEEK 48

Do not be anxious about anything, but in everything by prayer and supplication with thanksgiving let your requests be made known to God.

—PHILIPPIANS 4:6

LESSON TO LEARN

You can be a warrior, not a worrier.

DAY 1

Whatever you do, don't think about your favorite flavor of ice cream. I know—it's so refreshing and sweet, but don't think about it. Don't think about eating it with a spoon. Don't think about eating it out of a cone. Don't think about how much you want it for dessert tonight. So, what are you thinking about? Your favorite flavor of ice cream, right?

Maybe you've had thoughts like this. You keep worrying about something that you don't even want to be thinking about. Anxiety is on the rise in our world. No one is exempt. There are even toddlers experiencing anxiety. But while cases might be on the rise, anxiety isn't new.

Jesus preached about worry in Matthew 6:25–34. His solution to anxiety was to look at the world he created for us. The birds don't need to store food in barns because God, their Creator, provides food for them. Flowers are beautiful without giving any thought to their petals. God cares for birds and flowers, and they're not even his favorite part of creation. We are! If God takes care of birds and flowers, how much more does he want to take care of you?

As we learned from our ice cream experience, it's hard to just stop thinking about something. You probably won't stop thinking about ice cream until you replace the thought of ice cream with something else. We can replace our anxious thoughts too. But we must replace them with the right kinds of things. Here's the secret weapon against worry: gratitude. The next time you start to worry, make a list of all the things you're thankful for. Tell God about them. These positive thoughts will crowd out the negative ones.

CHALLENGE

Write a list of everything you're thankful for. Choose one thing from your list, and write a thank-you note to the person (or people) responsible for that thing.

DAY 2

Replace your anxious thoughts with gratitude and prayer.

MEMORY WORK

Do not be anxious about anything, but in everything by prayer and supplication with thanksgiving let your requests be made known to God.
—PHILIPPIANS 4:6

DAY 3

READ MATTHEW 6:25–34.

 How does God take care of his creation?

 What does God ask us to seek after? (Hint: look at verse 33.)

 How is worrying different from planning?

DAY 4

READ GENESIS 45:1–11.

 What are things Joseph's brothers could have worried about?

 Have you ever worried about something that never ended up happening?

 Why is worrying unproductive?

DAY 5

MENTORING MOMENT

MENTOR "What are some things you worry about? Is that worry helpful?"

CHILD "Is there ever a time that it's okay to worry?"

MENTOR "What are you thankful for?"

CHILD "How can I be better at showing gratitude?"

MENTOR "What does it look like to seek after the kingdom of heaven?"

CHILD "What helps you when you worry?"

CHALLENGE CHECK

How did the challenge go?
What did you learn?

WEEK 49

The things you have heard me say in the presence of many witnesses entrust to reliable people who will also be qualified to teach others.

—2 TIMOTHY 2:2, NIV

LESSON TO LEARN

God wants you to learn from those who have gone before you.

DAY 1

Do you have a teacher who has taken a special interest in you? Or have you ever had a coach who made you feel valued? Perhaps there is a pastor at your church who really, really cares about you. All these people are gifts from God who can make you better. That's how most leaders in the Bible got to be great—they were mentored by someone who went before them. A mentor is someone who can give you wisdom in a certain area of life because they have already been through it. People can have mentors in any area of their lives, including their careers, parenting, sports, and school. It's unlikely that one person could be knowledgeable in all these areas at once. As you grow, it's helpful to have multiple mentors.

You probably already have mentors built into your everyday life. You call them Mom and Dad. You'd be hard pressed to find another human that loves you and cares about your growth more. (If you're really lucky, you have an older sibling or grandparents that can give you some good guidance too.) They have been your age before. Maybe they didn't have the same technology or fashion, but they still dealt with a lot of the same things you're dealing with. And the biggest kicker of all . . . God gave you to them. And he doesn't make mistakes. He planned for them to be your parents because he knew what you needed.

CHALLENGE

Do some research on Walt Disney. What hard times did he face that helped him become better?

DAY 2

God has already placed people in your life to help guide you.

MEMORY WORK

The things you have heard me say in the presence of many witnesses entrust to reliable people who will also be qualified to teach others.
—2 TIMOTHY 2:2, NIV

DAY 3

READ 1 CORINTHIANS 11:1–3.

What do you think is the most important thing to look for in a mentor?

Why is it important to find a mentor who wants to be like Jesus?

Why does God put some people in positions of authority over others?

DAY 4

READ 2 TIMOTHY 2:1–13.

What could you do now to build endurance for when hard times come?

How can mentors help you through a hard time?

How does enduring through a hard time make you better?

DAY 5

MENTORING MOMENT

MENTOR "What's one area of life you would like a mentor in?"

CHILD "Whose influence on my life do you appreciate most?"

MENTOR "What mentors do you have right now?"

CHILD "How has a mentor made you better?"

MENTOR "How is God the ultimate mentor?"

CHILD "How will my needs for a mentor change as I grow up?"

CHALLENGE CHECK

How did the challenge go? What did you learn?

WEEK 50

HOW DO I MAKE SENSE OF THE BIBLE?

All Scripture is God-breathed and is useful for teaching, rebuking, correcting and training in righteousness, so that the servant of God may be thoroughly equipped for every good work.

—2 TIMOTHY 3:16–17, NIV

LESSON TO LEARN

God has given you tools to transform your life.

DAY 1

The Bible is a big book; it can be intimidating. It's also an old book, so it can be confusing. Let's start with some basic information that might make the Bible a bit easier to follow.

The Bible is divided into two main sections: the Old Testament and the New Testament. The word *testament* means "covenant" or "contract." (Go back to chapter 4 for a refresher.) The Old Testament followed an older set of guidelines. When Jesus came, in the New Testament, a new covenant was established.

In the front of your Bible, there should be a table of contents, which will tell you the page numbers of the book you're looking for. The book titles are also written on the top of the pages that they're on.

Once you find the book you're looking for, chapters and verses can help you find a reference quickly.

If you already have a plan in place for your daily Bible reading, great! Keep it up! If you don't, it's time. Here are a few steps to help you get started:

1. **Pick a place.** If you have a favorite cozy chair, that could work. If you prefer to sit at a desk, great! Pick a spot where you will read your Bible. You might be able to keep your Bible close to this place to make it even easier.
2. **Protect a time.** If you aren't a morning person, maybe night would work best. If you're busy a lot of nights, you may opt for the morning. It doesn't matter when you read your Bible. But you will be more likely to do it if you plan on doing it at the same time each day. Make it a goal to read at least four days a week.
3. **Grab a pen.** Keep a pen handy to write down questions as you read. You could keep all your thoughts in a journal, or you could even write questions in the margin of your Bible. Each day after reading, write the answer to two questions: (1) *What stood out to me in this passage?* (2) *How can I apply it to my life today?* You could also write down any questions to ask a parent or other mentor.

CHALLENGE

Make your plan for daily Bible reading. Pick a place, protect a time, and be consistent.

DAY 2

Make a Bible reading plan and stick to it.

MEMORY WORK

All Scripture is God-breathed and is useful for teaching, rebuking, correcting and training in righteousness, so that the servant of God may be thoroughly equipped for every good work.
—2 TIMOTHY 3:16–17, NIV

DAY 3

READ 2 TIMOTHY 4:1–8.

How does reading the Bible help your relationship with God?

Why is reading the Bible important if you're already learning the Bible at church?

What should you do if you don't understand something you read in the Bible?

DAY 4

READ EPHESIANS 6:10–18.

What parts of your body does God's armor protect?

God's armor is made up of several pieces. Most of the pieces are for defense. What's the one offensive weapon God has given us?

How can knowing the Bible protect you?

DAY 5

MENTORING MOMENT

MENTOR "What would you do to get to know a friend better? What should you do to get to know God better?"

CHILD "How do you spend time with God?"

MENTOR "What time of day are you most likely to spend time with God?"

CHILD "How has reading your Bible helped you know God better?"

MENTOR "How can you make Bible reading a habit?"

CHILD "How is the Bible helpful if it's so old?"

CHALLENGE CHECK

How did the challenge go?
What did you learn?

WEEK 51

HOW DO I GAIN GRIT?

Since we are surrounded by so great a cloud of witnesses, let us also lay aside every weight, and sin which clings so closely, and let us run with endurance the race that is set before us.

—HEBREWS 12:1

LESSON TO LEARN

You can do more than you think you can.

DAY 1

Many elementary schools have a physical health test. There's a stretch test to measure flexibility, a push-up test to measure strength, and a mile run to measure endurance. Many kids dread the mile run. You see, the other tests are over as soon as you decide to quit. But the mile run isn't over until you finish the mile. It requires grit—the attitude that says you refuse to give up, which can help you endure the really difficult stuff.

There are two types of mile runners in elementary school: people who run the whole mile and people who don't. Most people will start off running. But by the end of the mile, only a handful of students will still be running. The students who never walk will begin to pass the students who do. Many students who walk decide that the pain of the mile isn't worth pushing through. But in some ways their pain lasts longer because it takes them more time to finish. Students who push through understand that the true rest comes at the end of the mile.

You can get better at running if you want to! You just have to train your body to be able to run a little bit longer. It's called building your endurance. Some people even build their endurance to be able to run marathons. (That's 26.2 miles!) No one wakes up and decides to run a marathon that day. Marathon runners start by running one or two miles. It takes them months to train their bodies to be able to run a 26.2-mile race. They choose to train, even when they don't feel like it.

Did you know that in Hebrews 12:1–2 the Bible compares your life to running a race? How can you run that race well?

Realize that your reward isn't instant. You can get instant gratification by walking, but the real reward is finishing the race. A life with Jesus has its rewards here and now. But at the end of the race—at the end of your life—you will thank God that you endured.

Realize that there are consequences for quitting. The Bible is a helpful tool to expose what kinds of consequences our current behaviors will bring. Proverbs is an especially helpful book for this. There are thirty-one chapters in Proverbs and usually thirty-one days in a month. Read one chapter a day, and see what lessons you can learn from it.

Get over yourself. You're pretty great, but not as great as Jesus. He was perfect, and he dedicated his life to serving others, particularly people who couldn't offer him anything. Why don't you give it a try? Do something for someone without expecting anything in return.

Find a partner. Running with someone decreases the likelihood that you will walk. It encourages you and helps you realize that you're capable of more. We need partners in our lives too. Ask someone to be your accountability partner. Look for someone who will help you rise to the challenge and who will call you out when you need it.

Rest. Even the top athletes in the world have days of rest. Their bodies have been pushed to the limits. Their muscles need time to repair. Rest is as important to the training process as the training itself. Our lives are the same. God even modeled a day of rest after he created the earth. Spend a day detached from your normal technology and patterns, and fill that time with worship.

CHALLENGE

Run a mile this week. Think about how running a mile is like your life as a Christian.

DAY 2

Gaining grit requires training. Remember, you can do more than you think you can.

MEMORY WORK

Since we are surrounded by so great a cloud of witnesses, let us also lay aside every weight, and sin which clings so closely, and let us run with endurance the race that is set before us.

—HEBREWS 12:1

DAY 3

READ HEBREWS 11:24–29.

What did Moses give up? What did Moses gain?

What did Moses accomplish because he didn't give up?

Read Exodus 4:13–15. One of the ways to gain grit is to go find a partner. Who was Moses's partner, and what did he do to help?

DAY 4

READ PHILIPPIANS 3:7–11.

Have you ever given up a good thing to get something better?

What are the consequences of giving up early on something you've been working toward?

How is your Christian life like a long-distance race?

DAY 5

MENTORING MOMENT

MENTOR "Which training tip from this chapter do you need to work on?"

CHILD "What's one area of my life where I need to gain more grit?"

MENTOR "What's the hardest thing you've ever gone through?"

CHILD "When have you worked hard for something that had a delayed reward? Was it worth it?"

MENTOR "Who could be your partner in a difficult situation?"

CHILD "Why is grit developed in difficult situations?"

CHALLENGE CHECK

How did the challenge go? What did you learn?

WEEK 52

WHAT WILL HEAVEN BE LIKE?

I heard a loud voice from the throne saying, “Behold, the dwelling place of God is with man. He will dwell with them, and they will be his people, and God himself will be with them as their God.”

—REVELATION 21:3

LESSON TO LEARN

God is creating a fresh start for us.

DAY 1

According to this week's Scripture passage, God is going to give us a fresh start. His fingerprints are all over this earth. The sunset, the ocean, the mountains, and the wildflowers are all beautiful glimpses of heaven on earth. But in the midst of these heavenly glimpses, we also get glimpses of pain, loss, sickness, and evil. When something holds bad memories for us, sometimes it's helpful to throw it out and start over. While this earth might hold good memories, it also holds some very painful ones. God is going to make a new heaven and a new earth that won't hold any bad memories.

Another thing heaven won't hold is Satan. God wants you to make him king of your heart. But in order for you to make that choice, other choices must exist too. Otherwise, it's like asking someone what they want to drink when the only thing you have is water. On earth, God and Satan both exist, and a battle rages over our souls. God fights for you to serve him, and Satan fights for you to serve anything but God. When you choose to make God king of your heart, your reward is to be with him in heaven.

In heaven, there will be no more pain, no more tears, no more sadness, no more sickness, and no more evil. There will be unimaginable beauty and treasures. All the bad things will be removed, and all the good things will remain. There will even be some good things that we don't know about yet. All these things are great, but the real reason we want to go to heaven is that God is there. He is the reason we live. He is waiting to welcome us into the joy he has created for us. And we will get to live in this joy for eternity.

CHALLENGE

With your mentor, decide what you will do next for your spiritual development.

DAY 2

Heaven will be beautiful, new, and wonderful, but the best thing of all will be God's presence.

MEMORY WORK

I heard a loud voice from the throne saying, "Behold, the dwelling place of God is with man. He will dwell with them, and they will be his people, and God himself will be with them as their God."
—REVELATION 21:3

DAY 3

READ REVELATION 21:1–8.

What does God promise to give to his people?

What makes heaven so great?

Why is free choice necessary?

DAY 4

READ MATTHEW 7:13–14.

What do the narrow gate and wide gate represent?

What are some examples of the narrow road versus the wide road in our culture?

If God wants all people to make him king of their hearts, why is the road to heaven narrow?

DAY 5

MENTORING MOMENT

MENTOR "What would you like to have or do in heaven?"

CHILD "What do you want to ask God when you get to heaven?"

MENTOR "What's an example of a time you've chosen the narrow road?"

CHILD "What's one way you experience heaven on earth?"

MENTOR "What's the difference between doing good and following God?"

CHILD "What are ways I'm going to have to choose the narrow road as I get older?"

CHALLENGE CHECK

How did the challenge go?
What did you learn?

ABOUT THE AUTHORS

MARK E. MOORE is the acclaimed author of books such as *Core 52* and teaching pastor at Christ's Church of the Valley in Phoenix, Arizona—one of the fastest-growing and most dynamic churches in America. He previously spent two decades as a New Testament professor at Ozark Christian College. His passion is to make Jesus famous. Mark and his wife, Barbara, reside in Phoenix, Arizona.

MEGAN HOWERTON enjoys waking up early for her favorite treat: an Arizona sunrise. Megan is a veteran teacher who previously used her gifts as an elementary educator but now focuses on her favorite pupils, the Howerton children. *Core 52 Family Edition* was born out of combining her biggest passions—loving Jesus, raising the next generation, and valuable teaching. Megan lives in Phoenix with her husband and four wonderful children.

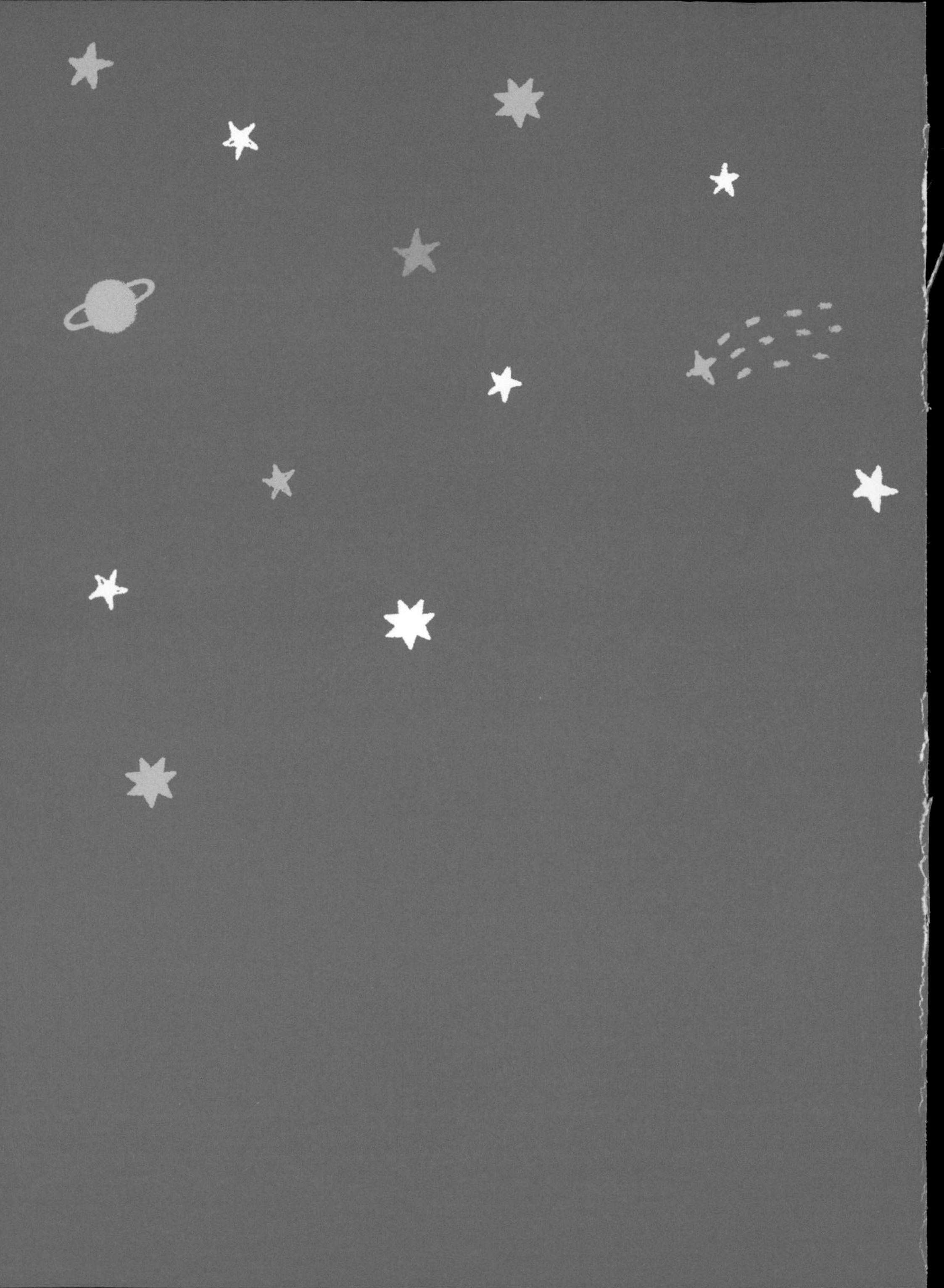